# SOCIAL AND LITERARY PAPERS

# SOCIAL

AND

# LITERARY PAPERS

BY

CHARLES CHAUNCY SHACKFORD

*Essay Index Reprint Series*

 **BOOKS FOR LIBRARIES PRESS**
FREEPORT, NEW YORK

First Published 1892
Reprinted 1972

Library of Congress Cataloging in Publication Data

Shackford, Charles Chauncy.
  Social and literary papers.

  (Essay index reprint series)
  CONTENTS: AEschylus on some modern social problems.
--A satirist in the second century.--A sceptic in the
eighteenth century. [etc.]
  1.  Social problems in literature--Addresses, essays,
lectures. 2.  Social problems--Addresses, essays,
lectures.  I.  Title.
PN51.S36  1972            814'.4              72-335
ISBN 0-8369-2825-3

PRINTED IN THE UNITED STATES OF AMERICA
BY
NEW WORLD BOOK MANUFACTURING CO., INC.
HALLANDALE, FLORIDA 33009

# NOTE.

THE Essays contained in this volume were pre-
pared for and read before various literary clubs
and societies, mostly in Boston and its vicinity.
Their printing was begun but a short time previous
to the death of the Author, the proofs of less than
one hundred pages having passed under his scru-
tiny. The work of editorial supervision was then
committed to the hands of Mr. A. W. STEVENS of
the University Press, who, in prosecuting the task,
has been studiously regardful of what he believes
would have been both the wish and the deed of the
Author.

In closing his work, the Editor cannot refrain
from expressing his hearty appreciation of the
great value and timeliness of many of the dis-
cussions carried on in these pages.

A. W. S.

APRIL, 1892.

# CONTENTS.

# SOCIAL AND LITERARY PAPERS.

## I.

### ÆSCHYLUS ON SOME MODERN SOCIAL PROBLEMS.

ÆSCHYLUS, the founder of the Greek lyric drama, possessed a soul severely grand like that of Milton, austerely just like that of Dante; and, like these poets, he too was drawn toward the religious, moral, and social problems of his time and of all time. These great masters of poetry are driven by a mighty wind; they are the voices of an uncounted multitude; and so must it be with all the great bards of the world's great literature.

No deeper problems occupy now the thought of mankind than those which make the contents of the "Prometheus" of Æschylus. There remains to us only one of the parts of this trilogy, — the second, or middle one, — and the structure can be completed only by inference; but what we have is enough to show the groundwork of the whole.

In the "Prometheus" is symbolized the progress of the human race; and under this statement we have a representation of the poet's view of man's relation to the universe, of the advance of culture and civilization, and of those problems of might and right, of justice and equality, of those eternal laws of progressive change for good, which it is the work to-day of science to establish for the satisfaction of man's reason and intellect.

According to the appearance that Nature presents to the first men, ignorant of any means of protection, of defence, — what is its aspect? Evidently, that of a hostile, tyrannical, merciless being, — now blasting with burning heat, now crystallizing with icy cold, now sending, according to his pleasure, the deadly arrows of pestilence, now sapping the strength by old age, and extinguishing all by death. In social life also are found might of arm and cunning of brain, securing to themselves wealth and power, and then plunged into the lowest wretchedness, — the ruler of a people begging his bread; the dweller in palaces an outcast in the desert, glad to find shelter in a cave, and share with the wild beast its prey. Man seems despised and hated by some higher powers. The gods envy his too great prosperity: they are indifferent to his good. Everywhere is the spectacle of triumphant might, — and of man, feeble, ignorant, suffering under numberless ills, dying from generation to generation, yet engaged in a hand-to-hand struggle with this seemingly irresistible force.

What must first free him? Knowledge, foresight, the divine spark within of aspiration and unconquerable will ; the never-resting desire to

better his condition, to find out all secrets, and
use for himself every divine force, every hidden
power. Whatever furthers this tendency to free
and help humanity is man's friend, man's bene-
factor, man's divine protector and champion.

With a different theory of the origin and progress of civilization from that which looked back
to an age of gold, and laid its paradise in some
far-off period of blessed innocence and of happy
contentment with the gods, Æschylus describes
the early condition of the human race as but just
removed from that of brutes : —

> " They dwelt
> In hollowed holes, like swarms of tiny ants
> In sunless depths of caverns ; and they had
> No certain signs of winter, nor of spring
> Flower-laden, nor of summer with her fruits.

And in another place he says, —

> " I, poor I, through giving
> Great gifts to mortal men, am prisoner made
> In these fast fetters ; yea, in fennel stalk
> I snatched the hidden spring of stolen fire,
> Which is to men a teacher of all arts,
> Their chief resource."

In Prometheus, then, is represented that grand
idea of a progressive culture, under the symbolic form of a Titanic contest with the Ruler
of the world, the Power that has seated itself by
mere force on the throne, and who hates the human race, so that he is willing to see it perish,
that its place may be supplied by creatures of his

own.  In the view of Æschylus, Zeus himself was
subject to a power which he must acknowledge, or
himself in turn be overthrown.  This power, moreover, was not the mere blank, rigid fate which is
often spoken of, — not the blind, irresistible chance
for which no one could account, and before which
each one must quake and tremble; but this power
was the Eternal Justice, the law of right, the everlasting balance, harmony, and proportion of all
things human and divine, which raised up the low
and cast down the high, which visited arrogance with
humiliation, which levelled every excess, and filled
up every hole and cranny of the universe with the
needed supply.  Prometheus boldly contended for
right against might, for the suffering against his
potent oppressor, for the vile worm against him
who trampled it in the dust.  He identified himself with the race of men, was their champion and
savior; and therefore he suffered.

    1. For the poet recognized the fundamental law
of all human growth and progress,— the law of
martyrdom,— and has embodied it in that godlike
form spiked to the bare Caucasus : —

> " Behold me bound, a god to evil doomed,
>     The foe of Zeus, and held
>     In hatred by all gods
>     Who tread the courts of Zeus :
>     And this for my great love,
>     Too great for mortal men."

This law of martyrdom is seen in the very constitution of the natural world.  Each successive

step of ascending life is gained by the rendering up of life in that which precedes; growth comes out of decay, life out of death. The earth is fertile because innumerable forms have lived and died. The solidest rock is crumbled into finest, impalpable powder ; the hardest mineral renders up its form, and, equally with the tenderest moss disintegrating at the touch, it becomes dissolved into dust; plants springing from these inhale the atmosphere and rains of heaven and ministering juices of the soil, and then give themselves up in turn to animal and man. Each higher form lives by the martyrdom of some lower, and death is everywhere the price of life. Is it any different in the moral and social spheres? Is not the present civilization of the world — its knowledge, art, comfort, well-being — the result of innumerable sorrows and deaths? Is not every stone of the foundation and every joint of the rising superstructure cemented by blood of the body, blood of the mind, blood of the very heart and soul of the noblest of the race in every age and among every people, from the earliest moment until this very hour in which we breathe our little lives? Not alone upon the battle-field, the gibbet, the cross, — not alone in dungeons and filthy prison-cells, have martyrs struggled and suffered for the good of man; but on sea and in the wilderness, in the workshop and the study, the pioneer of truth has swung his axe, has gazed into the heavens, has pored over the annals of the past, has delved and toiled, has despaired and hoped again, has seen the

stars rise and set, the sun pursue his daily course,
and seasons come and go, — still eager for the coming truth, watching for the new day, looking through
tearful eyes for a light that no mortal eye has ever
seen, a good that his own soul whispers shall one
day be the heritage of all his fellow-men.

This law of life Fichte has thus enunciated:

" Nothing individual can live in itself or for itself, but
all live in the whole ; and this whole unceasingly dies for
itself in unspeakable love, that it may rise again in new
life. This is the spiritual law : all that comes into being
falls a sacrifice to an eternally increasing and ascending
life ; and this law constantly rules over all, without waiting
for the consent of any. Here alone lies the distinction, —
whether man allow himself to be led, with the halter round
his neck, like a beast to the slaughter, or freely and nobly
brings his life a gift to the altar of the eternal life, in the full
fore-enjoyment of the life which is to arise from its ashes."

Does a man, then, really want to do good to
man? What must he look for? Martyrdom,—
that is, he must himself share in the suffering
that he would relieve; he must himself take upon
his own shoulders the burden he would remove.
The depth of his suffering must be in proportion
to the wretchedness he alleviates. The cup of
human woe, who can drink it off? Yet it must
be drunk off; and because it must, Zeus was called
tyrant, usurper, regardless of the welfare of the
race of men. So he *seemed* to the earliest rude
view; but this view recedes, and, as man sees the
real blessedness of the law, it is the law not of

death, but of life. Æschylus himself, in another drama, "The Suppliants," says, —

> "All that God works is effortless and calm;
> Seated on loftiest throne,
> Thence, though we know not how,
> He works his perfect will."

Again, the poet addresses him as "blest above all blessed ones," as —

> "Our Father, author of our life,
> Directing all his plans, —
> The great Master workman, Zeus."

All the great legends of mythology recognize this law, and thus show its universality. The hero, to save his country, must leap into the yawning chasm. The serpent cannot be slain unless its slayer receives a fatal hurt. The beleagured city can be taken, but the price of victory is the death of the beloved chief. To benefit man, the gods themselves must be incarnate, and share his daily life.

But more significant than all is this story of Prometheus, the god-descended lover of the miserable race of men, who brings to them fire, the arts, the gifts, which ennoble and bless humanity. But the price must be paid. His heart is devoured only to be perpetually renewed. The thunderbolt sinks him to Hades. He sinks, crying out, —

> "O Mother venerable!
> O Æther! rolling round,
> The common light of all,
> See ye what wrongs I bear?"

Have we any solution to this problem of the ages? Can we do good on any other terms? Be a reformer, if you will; but nothing will be reformed unless you bear in your own heart and mind and soul the evil you would remove. Work for the sorrowing, the debased, the oppressed, under any form, and the good will be in proportion to the bitter ingredients that fill one's own cup. By no high road of science have we yet escaped the operation of this universal necessity. The answer to the problem is found only in the higher law of love, which transforms the external pain into the highest spiritual blessedness.

In Prometheus the poet has symbolized humanity endowed with a divine spark of intelligence, raised by this above the brute, eager for all knowledge, resisting all demands that he shall unconditionally submit and bow himself in humility before the crushing might of Nature and natural forces, — believing, against all the threats of pain and all the wretchedness hurled upon his head, that he shall yet triumph and be blessed. Prometheus trusts in the prophetic utterance of his mother, Themis; that is, in righteous Order, holy Justice, harmonious Law.

The tender-hearted ocean-nymphs tell him he has sinned, though "a mist of fear and full of tears comes o'er their eyes." The rough but friendly Oceanus comes to advise him "to know himself and fit himself to words full new," to "humble himself and recognize in his suffering the punishment of his over-lofty speech." The facile Hermes, messenger of Zeus, bids him "be wise, and not to think that self-willed pride shall ever prove better than good counsel." The chorus, too, chants the beauty of implicit obedience to the enthroned power that rules by might, and not by right : —

> "Sweet is it in strong hope
> To spend long years of life,
> With bright and cheering joy
> Our heart's thoughts nourishing.
> I shudder, seeing thee
> Thus vexed and harassed sore
> By twice ten thousand woes ;
> For thou in pride of heart,
> Having no fear of Zeus,
> In thine own obstinacy,
> Dost show for mortal men
> Affection over-great,
> Prometheus, — yea, too great."

An eminent commentator, the Rev. Edward H. Plumptre, adds his voice to that of these poor comforters of the mighty sufferer, saying that Æschylus here embodied "the truth that the first result of the possession and the consciousness of enlarged powers is a new self-assertion, the spirit of independence and rebellion against the control of a divine order, the 'many inventions' that tend to evil, an outburst of impiety and lawlessness, needing the discipline of punishment before it can be brought round again into a nobler harmony."

How completely does this utterance chime with

2

the words put into the mouth of the chorus! "Rebellion against a divine order," "self-assertion,
many inventions tending to evil," says the English clergyman. "Pride of heart, having no fear
of Zeus," sang the temporizing chorus. How
much easier and sweeter to conform, to sign the
accepted creed, to enjoy what goods the present
ruling gods vouchsafe, than to follow the highest
inspiration, to do the good deed and speak the
protesting word that leads to social martyrdom!
"Rebellion against the control of a divine order."
Not such is the representation of Æschylus, whose
Zeus, in the "Prometheus," was only a divine order
*in the making*, not the father and maintainer of the
harmonious order of the world, whom he elsewhere
presents. The Greek god was in a process of evolution, as well as the Greek world and the Greek
man. Out of primeval chaos and night, out of the
contending powers of Nature and the fierce tendencies of men, was to be finally established that
law of which "no less is acknowleged than that
her seat is the bosom of God, her voice the harmony of the world, to whom all things in heaven
and earth do homage, the very least as feeling her
care, and the greatest as not exempted from her
power,— all, with uniform consent, admiring her
as the mother of their peace and joy."

Many, many ages were to pass away before this
could be established in the mind and heart of
the race. Meanwhile, humanity must suffer, and
could only be redeemed by "self-assertion," by

protest against unjust might, against every form
of evil and wrong; by the suffering of those
content to renounce "bright and cheering joys,"
and in what friends often, as well as foes, pronounce a spirit of rebellion, maintaining unflinch-
ingly their own independence, their own deepest
inspiration.

What does that leader of all conservatism — the
Papal power — say to-day of the progress of science,
the speculations of the intellect, and the investi-
gations into Nature's laws? "It is an ungodly
spirit of rebellion against the control of a divine
order;" it is "a restless spirit of dissatisfaction
that seeks out 'many inventions;'" it is "that
unholy curiosity which would be wise above what
is written, and which is leading men — a deceptive
will-o'-the-wisp — into the swamps of worldliness
and utter despair." The divine spark is not in
humanity, but in the Church. The inspiration of
God is not in the hearts of men, but in an established organization. The salvation is not in knowledge, but in faith. The praiseworthy act is not to
seek the well-being and happiness of man, but to
acquiesce, without murmuring, in the commands of
the mighty Zeus.

Such, under modified forms, is everywhere the
same warning of a timorous conservatism. Whoever distrusts human reason; whoever fears the
advance of humanity in all that relates to the
principles of equality, justice, and truth; whoever
believes that man must be forever kept down by

authority, by appeals to fear, and by manacles of restraint, — whoever he may be, and under whatsoever name he may intrench himself, he belongs to that class who would say to Prometheus in the words of the shifty Hermes, —

> "Search well, be wise, nor think that self-willed pride
> Shall ever better prove than counsel good.

2. In Æschylus further is to be found that principle of which we hear so much at the present day, — the law of heredity; a law as absolute as fate, destiny, irresistible necessity. The doom hovers over a race. The terrible and avenging Furies cannot be escaped, because not merely the ancient crime, but the ancient *tendency to crime*, survives, and at last works out the final retribution, — the purification of the evil stain from the earth. The evil-doer fills up the cup of sin; and not until he does fill this up freely, and from the groundwork of his own self-determined will, does the fearful vengeance descend upon his head. Thus the chorus chants in the Oresteia: —

> "Because of blood that mother earth has drunk,
> The guilt of slaughter that will vengeance work
> Is fixed indelibly;
> And Ate, working grief,
> Permits awhile the guilty one to wait,
> That so he may be full and overflow
> With all-devouring ill."

No! with him there is no background of causeless fatality from which there is no escape, and

which works at random with its fearful hurling of
the thunderbolt at a venture.

Neither does he give that older view of the gods
as envying the too great prosperity of a mortal
man, whom therefore they thrust down from his
lofty pinnacle of happiness. Only as riches and
power brought with them arrogance and lawless
freedom in evil, only as presumptuous insolence
followed upon unmeasured prosperity, did the unsleeping eye of a righteous justice strike down and
annihilate the offender. What can be clearer in
statement than the choral strophe, —

> " There lives a saying, framed in olden days,
>   In memories of men, that high estate
>   Full grown brings forth its young, nor childless dies ;
>   And that from great success
>   Springs to the race a woe insatiable.
>   But I, apart from all,
>   Hold this my creed alone :
>   That impious act it is that offspring breeds,
>   Like to their parent stock ;
>   For still in every house
>   That loves the right, their fate for evermore
>   Hath issue good and fair."

Yes; man inherits the tendencies to vice, to
evil-doing, to insanity, to drunkenness, to folly,
as well as tendencies to virtue, to right-doing and
right-feeling, to purity and moral strength. The
old poet has not misinterpreted or misapplied the
great social law that lies at the basis of much of
the philanthropic effort of tò-day. He has echoed
and re-echoed its fearful truth; and so much of a

remorseless fate as lurks in the assertion of the modern philanthropist, the modern scientific statist, so much and no more pervades his stately verse.   No more of a fate, blind and resistless, hovers with black wings over his rhythmical page than over that of Shakspeare.   In both we can clearly read the law of heredity, and the overruling powers of justice and of right.   In both are presented the same essential facts; but they are presented from different sides,— in Æschylus from the divine, and in Shakspeare from the human side; but in both is the working out of the same harmonious order, the restoring of the same equal balance of unerring retribution.   In neither can any hopeful struggle be made against the higher decrees of wisdom, order, justice, and truth.   In Shakspeare we see that no man can flee from himself; in Æschylus, that no man can flee from Zeus: —

> " Hard are these things to judge :
>     The spoiler shall be spoiled,
>     The slayer pay his debt;
>     Yea, while Zeus liveth through the ages, this
>     Lives also, — that the doer bear his deed ;
>     For this is Heaven's decree.
>     Who now can drive from out the kingly house
>     The brood of curses dark ?
>     The house to Ate *cleaves.*"

*That* is why she cannot be driven out, because the house cleaves to her, and not because she cleaves to the house.

Matthew Arnold, quoting this passage from

Davison, "Conscience and the present constitution of things are not corresponding terms: it is conscience and the *issue* of things which go together," remarks : —

"It is so ; and this is what makes the spectacle of human affairs so edifying and so sublime. The world goes on, nations and men arrive and depart with varying fortune, as it appears, with time and chance happening unto all. Look a little deeper, and you will see that one strain runs through it all : nations and men, whoever is shipwrecked is shipwrecked on *conduct.* It is the God of Israel steadily and irresistibly asserting himself, — *the Eternal that loveth righteousness.*"

What is this but another expression of the Greek poet's view : "While Zeus liveth through the ages, this lives also, — that the doer bear his deed "? What but an echo, from a different summit, of that strain which runs through all humanity, because in humanity there is one inspiring life?

3. To-day, again, we have the problem discussed of the accumulation and distribution of wealth; but it is not new. The particular form under which it comes is adapted to our age; but the instability of that wealth gained by unjust means, by means that disturbed the harmony of the social order, was loudly proclaimed by our poet, making the burden of many a chorus. He speaks of the vision of truth which is manifest to the children

"Of those who, overbold,
Breathed raging war beyond the bounds of right;

Their houses *over*filled with precious store
Above the golden mean.
For still there is no bulwark strong in wealth
Against destruction's doom,
To one who, in the pride of wantonness,
Spurns the great altar of the Right and Just."

Ah, well! there are other means to-day of ac-
cumulating unjust wealth, of towering above the
golden mean, besides laying under contribution
friendly cities, and sacking the rich strongholds
of neighboring allies. There are unjust monopo-
lies, grinding oppressions of capital and machinery, vast, legalized means of sucking up the life-
blood of the community, by which millions upon
millions are piled up for the few, while the great
mass is sunk in poverty, vice, and ignorance. Oh
for some Æschylus to thunder out in his majestic
chorus, —

"And the dark-robed Erinnys, in due time,
By adverse chance of life,
Place him who prospers through unrighteousness
In gloom obscure ; and once among the unseen,
There is no help for him.
Fame in excess is but a perilous thing ;
For on men's quivering eyes
Is hurled by Zeus the blinding thunderbolt.
I praise the good success
That rouses not God's wrath."

The children find out. Yes! Is not that true of
thousands of our richest men, whose children pass
miserable lives of selfish egoism, cynical in their
excess of idle luxury, killing time as they can in
amateur nothings, — weary of themselves, weary of

the world, even if not steeped in drunkenness and vice? Alas for the children of those whose houses are "*over*filled with precious store above the golden mean,"—that golden mean which, through a wise and just distribution by means of a true science of economy and an organization of industry and all social appliances, might be the heritage of all. Another age, looking through a purer medium, shall brand many of our present arrangements and institutions as unrighteous as were those Athenian military expeditions,—so honorable then, so enriching to those who signalized themselves by cunning stratagem, by valorous deed, by a marvellous success.

4. Again, the social science of to-day busies itself with the question of health. The poet propounds the same problem:—

> " Of high, o'erflowing health
>   There is no limit fixed that satisfies ;
>   For evermore disease, as neighbor close
>   Whom but a wall divides,
>   Upon it presses ; and man's prosperous state
>   Moves on its course and strikes
>   Upon an unseen rock."

This unseen rock science would get the soundings of, and mark its place upon the chart, even if it cannot, by means of gunpowder or yet more explosive substance, blow it to atoms. Chance, fate, necessity, no more rules there than it does in the lives and fortunes of men. But this the poet did not see. How many see it now? How many recognize health as the normal state, the

possible possession of all, and disease as the self-
imposed burden of ignorance and sin,— that inherited curse which shall last only so long as the
house cleaves to Ate; only so long as man, by his
own wilful folly and voluntary transgression, in-
vites the company of the avenging Fates?

5. Again, among the problems of to-day there
is none more striking than that of the union of
those who think themselves suffering great social
wrongs, and who in their union find solace and
strength. The great law of human fellowship, of
like experience and a common destiny, binds them
together. The fact itself is a significant sign;
and the occasional excesses of a new-found strength
should not blind us to the real importance and the
essential necessity, in an advancing civilization, of
this brotherhood of the suffering, this voicing of
their complaints. Where is their hope, if not in
themselves? It is, too, for the advantage of all
that every wrong shall be righted, every evil removed; that every faculty of every human being for
enjoyment and improvement shall be unfolded to
its full capacity and its utmost extent. Grudge
not, then, this fellowship of suffering, aspiration,
and effort. The ancient poet, by the intuition of
genius, brings together from remote parts of the
earth the two colossal sufferers by the tyranny of
Zeus, — the frenzy-smitten Io and the tortured
Prometheus. By an unconscious and invisible attraction, Io is brought to the rock to which the
indomitable sufferer is nailed, and exclaims, —

> " Ah, who of all that suffer, born to woe,
>   Have trouble like the pain that I endure ?
>   But thou make clear to me
>   What yet for me remains, —
>   What remedy, what healing, for my pangs.
>   Show me, if thou dost know ;
>   Speak out and tell to me,
>   The maid by wanderings vexed."

Prometheus unfolds the future to her by prophetic insight, and describes to her the course and
ending of her untold torments, urging her to unfold "the tale of her great woe," saying,—

> " To bewail and moan one's evil chance
>   Here where one trusts to gain a pitying tear
>   From those who hear, — this is not labor lost."

It is a human touch which might, one would think,
justify itself even to those purblind critics who
call this an episode, and who would, had they been
consulted, have created a better poem than that of
Æschylus ! But it needs no justification as an
integral and vital part of the perfect fabric. It
is the symbolic cry of the human heart for some
sympathy with its woes, of that suffering in common which makes the whole world kin.

By the same sympathetic bond the strong Titan
is drawn towards other sufferers. In the midst
of his own pangs, he says : —

> " Lo ! my mind is wearied with the grief
>   Of that my kinsman, — Atlas, — who doth stand
>   In the far west, supporting on his shoulders
>   The pillars of the earth and heaven, — a burden

His arms can ill but hold.   I pity, too,
The giant dweller of Kilikian caves,
A helpless, powerless carcase, near the strait
Of the great sea, fast pressed beneath the roots
Of ancient Ætna."

Yes: towards all these whom "the unsleeping
thunder-bolt of Zeus" has struck down he is drawn
with tenderest pity.   So, on the bare heath, with
the thunder bursting around him, and amidst the
flashings of lightning and the tempest, the crazed
Lear, before he accepts the shelter of the miserable hovel, expresses the new feeling of sympathy
with the wretched : —

"Poor, naked wretches, wheresoe'er you are
That bide the pelting of this pitiless storm,
How shall your houseless heads and unfed sides,
Your looped and windowed raggedness, defend you
From seasons such as these ?   Oh, I have ta'en
Too little care of this.   Take physic, Pomp !
Expose thyself to feel what wretches feel,
That thou may'st shake the superflux to them,
And show the heavens more just."

The heavens more just?   Are the bountiful heavens
to blame?   Is not the earth fertile, and the means
of good sufficient for all?   When the superflux shall
be wisely distributed, will that dumb sorrow which
pains so many hearts be turned into gladness, and
those muttered curses that well up from so many
quivering souls be changed into benedictions.

   6.  The last problem brought under our view is
that of labor, — by many, indeed, regarded as *the*

question which transcends all others, and which
concerns more immediately and more intimately
the well-being of humanity. What has Æschylus
to do with that? Is *that* embraced under his grand,
symbolic picture? Why not? His theme in the
"Prometheus" is the godlike element in man, —
its protests, its struggles, and its final triumph;
and how could it be that this force, labor, the application of man's strength of arm, of his power
to work, of the employment of muscular vigor and
all his bodily energies, — that this great necessity
should not enter into his view? Humanity, or
Prometheus with his unbending will, his far-reaching intelligence, his reckless love, is freed from
the bird of Jove that daily feeds upon his liver by
Hercules, whose heroic title was the labor of his
own strong arm, his broad chest, his brawny muscles, his thick neck. He slays the ravaging lion,
the venomous hydra, the savage wild boar, the
death-dealing birds, the carnivorous monsters;
cleanses the Augean stables, and finally brings
up from hell itself its fearful guardian. Intelligence by itself alone is fettered, is powerless; but
intellect and labor combined are the essentials of
human progress. And how was this labor-hero,
this god of work, equipped for his task? He received his helmet from Minerva, his sword from
Mercury, his horse from Neptune, his arrows from
Apollo, and his golden cuirass from Vulcan. That
is, labor — endowed, equipped, furnished with the
gifts, the graces, the appliances of art, of commerce,

of intelligent skill — frees humanity from its evils and its foes in the air above and on the earth, and even from the hell under the earth.

In the concluding part of the dramatic trilogy of "Prometheus," the heroic Titan, after thousands of years, becomes reconciled with a reconciled Zeus, and sits down with the Olympian gods at a grand marriage feast in the abode of the Immortals, — the highest symbol that the inspired imagination can set forth of the glory and blessedness of a race redeemed by knowledge, redeemed by labor; every faculty, every aspiration, every work, made blessed and divine.

# II.

## A SATIRIST IN THE SECOND CENTURY.

Lucian lived in the age of the Antonines, in the second century of our era, — an age which Gibbon has pronounced to be the one that he should select as the most prosperous and happy of all the historical ages of the world. On the surface it looks so. It was a time of external order, of general, peaceful intercourse, and of great cities in the East and the West, — from Egypt to Gaul, — with schools of philosophy and art, where letters were cultivated, and refinement was the fashion.

Among the literary men of that age, none stands more prominent than Lucian of Samosata, the capital of the northern province of Syria, on the western side of the river Euphrates, whose inhabitants spoke the Grecian language. Lucian, an accomplished scholar, wrote almost pure classic Greek. Educated to the law, in his mature years he accumulated a large fortune by his lectures on philosophy, literature, and religion. A genuine product of his times, he reveals them to us better than could any historical essay. He shows that it was a period of general dissolution of the old religions, and that the soil was ready to receive a new positive faith, — that Christianity required no

miracles to make it flourish, but found everywhere
congenial helps.

Lucian was the great satirist of his time; he
laughed at religion, at philosophy of every sect
and kind.  He believed neither in God nor philosophers, and covers every sacred rite, every
philosophical school, every tradition of the gods,
and every theoretical speculation in regard to a
divine existence and future life with unrestrained
ridicule.  He has been called the Voltaire of his
age; but he is rather the Robert Ingersol raised
to the $n$th power.

Let us transport ourselves into the Roman province of Syria, about the year 135 of our Christian
era.  An inhabitant of the city of Samosata is holding a family council to see what shall be done with
a smart, lively, and promising boy, about fifteen
years of age, who has received the usual elementary
education, and must now be turned to something
which shall give him a living.  It was a trouble-
some question then, as it is now, what to do with
an irrepressible young fellow; but it was finally
concluded to put this one to some mechanical
trade.  But what trade?  Most of the common
occupations were filled by slaves, and this was a
freeman's son.  He had already shown some dex-
terity in shaping figures out of wax,— for which
his schoolmaster had often boxed his ears; and
so the father, turning to the maternal uncle of the
boy, a stone-cutter and sculptor, said: "It would
be affronting you to give the preference to any

other art; so take the boy, and do the best you can
with him."

This decision strikes the youth favorably, for he
thinks it will be a very fine thing to carve little
gods and goddesses for himself and his playmates.
His uncle puts a chisel into his hand and sets him
to work on a slab of marble, which he soon succeeds in breaking, and receives therefor a sound
whipping. Smarting with pain and boiling over
with rage, the boy goes for comfort to his mother,
and under her soothing influence he falls asleep.
He dreams that two forms, one of whom is Statuary and the other Learning, appear and quarrel
for the mastery of his person. Each presents her
case; and after the first has depicted the solid advantages of a life of labor, Learning thus speaks:

"You already know my countenance, but much is still
wanting to complete the acquaintance. If you follow this
low person, you will be nothing more than a mechanic, be
paid little better than a day-laborer, low and narrow in
your views, an insignificant personage in the commonwealth, a mere handicraftsman, — one of the vulgar herd,
bowing and cringing to his superiors, adopting the opinion of every speaker, and living the life of a timid hare.
Follow me, and I will make you acquainted with all the
admirable characters of antiquity, and give you a complete knowledge of all things human and divine. You,
the poor lad now standing before me, the son of a common man who would bring you up to such an ignoble
trade, will shortly be envied by every one; for you will
be commended, honored, and esteemed as a man of ex-

3

cellent talents. You will be dressed as you see me here, and every one who sees you will jog his neighbor, point to you and say: 'There he goes! that is the famous Lucian!' Think of that great Demosthenes, whose son he was, and what a man I made of him! Was not Eschines the son of a woman who played on a kettle-drum? Socrates was brought up to statuary, but he soon made a better choice; and you know how much he has been magnified by all men. And would you reject all this to go sneaking about in a coarse canvas frock, always handling iron tools, and poring over your work with both body and mind pinned fast to the ground?"

Such was the substance of a public lecture which Lucian delivered to his townsmen many years afterward, when he returned to his native place with a splendid retinue, after he had amassed a fortune in the practice of the law, and had visited many cities of the vast Roman empire as a lecturer on Rhetoric and Belles Lettres. Most of his writings are in the form of dialogue, — a form which Plato sanctioned, and which became very common.

The mythological dialogues exhibit the absurdities of the popular beliefs in a lively and a grotesque way, attacking no one's faith, and yet covering the entire Olympus with ridicule. The stories of the gods were received as literal facts by all except a few allegorizing philosophers: as literal facts they are dealt with on Lucian's part, and a sorry figure enough do the gods cut. They enact over again in the author's page their most vulgar and licentious parts; they exhibit all the low passions that the lowest human beings could in performing the same actions; they scold and lie; they slander and ridicule; they reproach and jeer; they flatter and betray one another in the most bare-faced manner, and not a shred of what is sacred or venerable remains for the motley crew.

In the mythologic story, Jupiter has abducted the beautiful boy Ganymede, and borne him to Olympus, where, according to Lucian, this conversation takes place between them: —

*Jupiter.* Now, my dear Ganymede, we are come to our journey's end. Kiss me, you fine little fellow! There, you see I have no crooked beak now, no sharp claws and no wings, as you thought I had, when I looked like a bird.

*Ganymede.* How! You surely were not the eagle that came flying down, and bore me away from my flock? Where did you get your wings, and what makes you look so different now?

*Jupiter.* Oh, my fine boy, I am neither a man nor an eagle. I am the king of the gods, who took the form of an eagle to carry out my design.

*Ganymede.* What! You are Pan, then? But where's your pipe, and your horns and your goat's feet?

*Jupiter.* Do you think there are no gods except him?

*Ganymede.* In our village we don't know any other, and we sacrifice a whole he-goat before the cave where his image stands. Perhaps you are one of those bad men who steal people and sell them into slavery!

*Jupiter.* Do tell me if you have never heard of Jupiter,

and never seen on the top of Ida the altar of the god who sends rain, lightning, and thunder?

*Ganymede.* It was you then who lately pelted us so fiercely with hail-stones, and who made such a clattering up among the clouds, and to whom my father sacrificed a ram! But what have you flown off with me for? My sheep will run wild, and be torn to pieces by the wolves.

*Jupiter.* Why should you bother yourself about the silly sheep? You are now immortal, and will stay with us.

*Ganymede.* What! shall I not be taken back to Ida to-day?

*Jupiter.* Of course not. What did I turn myself from a god into an eagle for?

*Ganymede.* But my father will be angry, and I shall be beaten for having left my sheep.

*Jupiter.* He shall not see you again.

*Ganymede.* I will go home! If you'll carry me back, I promise that he shall sacrifice to you another ram, — the big three-year old that always goes at the head of the flock.

*Jupiter.* How simple-minded and ingenuous the boy is! My dear Ganymede, you must think no more of such things. You shall be my cup-bearer, and instead of milk and cheese, eat ambrosia and drink nectar. You shall be an immortal, and a star with your name shall sparkle in the sky. In short, you shall be very happy.

*Ganymede.* But who will play with me? I used to have many playfellows on Mt. Ida.

*Jupiter.* Oh, I will give you heaps of playthings, and Cupid shall be your play-fellow. So cheer up, and don't fret about things below.

Thus it goes on.

As having many points of resemblance to what has taken place in our own day, the account which Lucian, in the second century, gives us of one Alexander of Abonoteichos is full of interest. Alexander was a handsome youth, with commanding figure, bright eyes, and a musical gift, and at the same time noted for his many licentious adventures, — so that when a travelling physician and conjurer came around who wanted an assistant, this same prepossessing youth seemed made specially to his hand. His master soon died, and Alexander set up in business for himself, choosing for the beginning of his career the city of Chalcedon, where he buried in an old dilapidated temple of Apollo two brass plates, on which was inscribed: "Æsculapius will shortly come with his father Apollo into Pontus, and fix his abode at Abonoteichos." Of course the tablets were found in due time; and the prepossessing Alexander, with flowing ringlets, white vest striped with purple, a long white mantle, and holding a scimitar in his right hand, *à la* Perseus, — for he claimed to be directly descended by his mother's side from that hero, — appeared in the marketplace. All the population turned out for the show. After foaming at the mouth, and uttering a rhapsody in which the names of Apollo and Æsculapius were frequently heard, Alexander suddenly started for the temple; went to the fountain, and there took up an egg, out of which crept a little snake, that the people all hailed as the god

Æsculapius. The entire country was stirred up; and Alexander, with a fine, large, tame snake in his bosom, made an almost triumphal progress through the land. What a prodigious miracle was here! What a crowding and squeezing into the little room where Alexander in his grand attire fondled the newly manifested god! Medals were struck off, brass and silver figures of the new divinity were distributed, to whom the name Glycon was given by express command.

It was given out now that the god would deliver oracles and make prophecies, and a day was set when people should bring their scrolls carefully sealed into the temple, when the prophet would hand them back with an answer in metrical form to each. The people all said, "How could this man know what was inside the scrolls unless he were a god!" The throngs increased, the gains were immense. After a while, some opposition beginning to show itself, the prophet denounced the unbelievers as atheists, Christians, and Epicureans. Greater wonders are contrived; the head of the serpent speaks. The renown of the oracle extends to Rome, and the most eager to consult it were people of rank and wealth. Rutillianus, a man in high command, consults the prophet in regard to the education of his son, and to the question who shall be his tutors receives this answer: "Pythagoras and the greatest bard of warriors." The boy died suddenly a few days after this, and the father saw herein the fulfilment of the oracle, — which had evidently recommended, not any living tutor, but Homer and Pythagoras, whose instructions he could now receive. The old Rutillianus now consults the oracle in regard to marrying again, and is told to take "Alexander's and Selene's daughter for his wife." This the prophet interprets as meaning his own daughter, whose descent he traced from Selene, or the moon; and Rutillianus celebrates the espousals in splendid style.

The prophet is now resorted to from every part of the Roman empire. He institutes mysteries with torch bearers, processions, priests, etc.; and by public proclamation all atheists, Christians, and Epicureans are warned to keep away. The atheists of course would despise them, the Christians abhor them as the work of evil spirits, and the Epicureans laugh at them as morbid fancies and foolish trickeries. In these mysteries were represented the birth of Apollo and Æsculapius, the loves of Luna and the new Endymion, and the birth of Glycon. In the mystical torch-dance the prophet figured, and as his dress flew open there was visible a golden thigh. Beautiful young girls of noble birth came to chant hymns to the newly manifested god. Those women whom the prophet honored with a kiss were thought to be specially blest. Lucian says that he himself consulted the oracle, proposing, in a billet sealed up in such a way that it could not be opened without detection, the following weighty question: "Is Alexander bald?" The answer received the next night was this: "Atlis was a different king from Sbardala-chus." Another time the sceptic asked what country Homer belonged to; and having instructed his servant to hint that his master wished for a remedy for a pain in his side, the answer came in due form: "Anoint thee with citmis and Latona's dew." Another time he asked the same question, hinting to his servant that it was about an intended journey to Italy; and the response was: "Beware of the sea, travel only by land." Lucian came near paying very dear for his unmasking of the impostor, as this model spiritualist bribed the crew of a vessel in which Lucian took passage to throw him into the sea; and this intended disposition of the unbeliever was thwarted only by the resistance of the captain. But Alexander had influence enough at court to procure a decree of the emperor that a new coin should be struck, having on one side the serpent of Æsculapius, with the inscription, "Abonoteichiton Glukon;" and on the other, "Ionopoleiton Glukon," with the inscription, "Luc. verus." He had prophesied that he should live to be one hundred and fifty years old, and be struck by lightning; but he died before he was seventy, of a horrible gangrene. After his death there was a lively contest who should be his successor; but Rutillianus decided that the deceased did not abdicate by his death his prophetic office.

What a light is here thrown upon the surging of that human heart of the second century! "Human weakness and credulity!" some one exclaims. But what a longing for something beyond what time and sense can give! The sacred longings, the divine instincts, are imposed upon and misled; but what a capacity it argues in man that he can be thus deceived, thus mocked, thus put off with the semblance of the true food, and ever hope on for that light to come from above, and that word to be spoken, which shall cause him to bend in reverential awe! We see here a glimpse of that spiritual capacity, which, once set free from poly-theistic superstition, would accept the substance of Christian truth under modified forms, adapted, indeed, to its low mental and moral state. But humanity is not left wholly without God in the world; it subsides neither into atheistic materialism, nor epicurean carelessness and ease.

In another work, a jolly fellow, Menippus, flying with the wings of an eagle and a vulture, takes his station far above the earth, upon which he looks down and moralizes. Wearied with the contradictory explanations of the philosophers, the bold Menippus determines to find out by actual inspection the condition of other worlds; but his attention is chiefly fixed upon this earth. From his elevation all Greece appeared to be about four fingers in breadth, and the territories for which thousands of brave men were fighting no bigger than an Eygptian bean. The cities were like ant-hills, where there was nothing but bustle, running round, posting in and out, hurrying and scudding, one with a bean and another with a barley-corn in his mouth.

Menippus pays a visit to Jupiter, with whom he goes to the place where the god listened to the prayers of mankind. There were apertures, like well-mouths, provided with covers, and by the side of each a golden chair of state. Jupiter seated himself and lifted up the cover, and Menippus stooped down so that he could hear also. Various were the prayers: —

"O Jupiter, let me be king!"
"O Jupiter, make my onions and garlic thrive!"
"O Jupiter, help me get rid of my wife!"
"Give success to my law-suit!"
"Crown me at Olympia!"

One sailor prays for a north wind, another for a south; a farmer asks for rain, and a fuller for sunshine. Jupiter heard them all, and deposited some requests on the right hand, and others he puffed away. In regard to one only was he puzzled, and that was where two persons presented exactly opposite petitions, promising precisely the same sacrifices. Here he was forced to suspend his judgment, simply remarking, "We shall see." Menippus is entertained with the best of fare, and finally falls asleep wondering how Apollo could live to be as old as he was and have no beard, and how it could be night in heaven since the sun was there carousing with them. Early

in the morning Jupiter summons a council of the
gods, to consult them about the philosophers, —
"a mere set of declaimers, who, if they were asked
what they were good for, what they contributed to
the general welfare, each would be obliged to say,
'Although I neither till the ground, nor carry on
trade, nor perform military service, nor exercise
any profession, yet I find fault with everybody,
live sordidly, bathe in cold water, go barefoot in
winter, and carp at the doings of everybody else.'"
The assembly cries out with one voice that they
must be exterminated, and Jupiter promises that
they shall be gored to death on the horns of their
own dilemmas. After a while Menippus's wings
are clipped, and he is set down upon the earth.

In Lucian are to be found the originals of many
of those burlesque and gigantesque stories which
supply so much amusement to us as youthful readers, and which have so many sharp points of satire
that we are luckily blind to, until knowledge of
the evil itself has made us wiser if not happier.
Such a piece is the Dream of Micillus, or the
Cock. The poor cobbler Micillus is awakened
before light from a dream of riches by the crow-
ing of a cock. He threatens to kill the creature
as soon as he can see; but to his utter amazement
the bird addresses him. Micillus expresses his
surprise; but the cock asks whether that is such
a mighty miracle, — whether Achilles's horse did
not declaim a great number of hexameters; if the

ship Argo did not talk, the famous beech of Do-
dona's grove deliver oracles, and the oxen of the
sun low after they were roasted? The cock de-
clares that he had passed through many transmigra-
tions, and had once been Pythagoras. He recounts
the various experiences he had been through as a
rich man and as a king, with all their annoyances,
vexations, conspiracies, hatreds, and reverses, —
"favorites out of humor, mistresses false, conspiracies hatched, and, worst of all, not being able
to trust one's bosom friend and nearest relatives."
The cobbler is sufficiently cured of his hankering
after wealth, to exclaim, "Enough! enough! If
all this is true, I'd rather break my back in stoop-
ing over my lap stone, and cut leather into strips,
than drink poison out of a golden goblet. The
worst that can happen to me is to cut my finger
with a paring-knife, and I can cure that with a
cobweb."

But the poor cobbler cannot get wholly rid of
the desire to be rich. Especially is his envy excited by one Simon, a man now rolling in luxury,
who was once as poor as himself. The cock has
been endowed by Mercury with the power of opening any door, and seeing without being seen; and
so they visit — like "le diable boiteux," of Le
Sage — a great many dwellings, where the inmates
think themselves safe and sound from observation.
First to the envious Simon's, whom they find sitting wide awake and poring over his accounts.
He soliloquizes: "Those seventy talents I have

hidden safe under my bed; but I am afraid that
Sosylus saw me hide those sixteen behind the
manger. My plate is not safe in this cupboard.
I have a great many enviers and enemies; especially, I have no faith in Micillus, that neighbor
of mine. I will go round the house and see if
all's safe." He now stumbles against a statue,
but on striking it perceives his mistake; he counts
his gold again, and is startled out of his wits by
some fancied noise. The cobbler says that on
these conditions he would be willing to have all
his enemies rich. Other houses are visited, and
the cobbler comes to the conclusion that he would
rather starve than be like these persons whom he
had so greatly envied.

Another work by Lucian is entitled "The True
History," intended as a match for all the wonderful stories of travellers and mythologists, which
were undoubtedly so rife in that unhistorical and
credulous time. He proposes to cure those who
are rabid by giving them a hair of the very dog
that bit them, outdoing the adventures of the
wandering Ulysses.

The narrator setting out in a vessel from
Cadiz, with fifty companions, after having been
driven before the wind for eighty days, came to
pillars inscribed: "Thus far came Bacchus and
Hercules." Then, going farther on by land, they
came to a large navigable river, which ran wine
instead of water,— a striking confirmation of the

fact that Bacchus had visited that region. They also saw women whose fingers and hair terminated in vines and bunches of grapes. They returned to the ship, which was taken up by a whirlwind and carried along above the clouds, until they came to a large, shining, circular island, to which they moored the vessel. Here they were seized by some men riding on huge vultures, and carried before the king, who was no other than Endymion. This lunar king was at war with Phæton, the solar king, and the strangers accompany their host the next day to the battle. Such troops an unbridled imagination never collected before! Falstaff himself would have been outfaced by such a regiment! — eighty thousand on huge vultures, and twenty thousand on birds, who were thickly grown over with cabbages instead of feathers, with wings of lettuce-leaves; archers mounted on fleas three times as large as elephants; and wind-coursers, who wore long gowns, which they tucked up and used as sails. The horse-cranes and other terrible troops which were to come he cannot describe, for he did not see them, — as they never came. Some spiders in the moon, the smallest of which was larger than the biggest of the Cyclades, were ordered to fill up the whole tract between the moon and the morning star with a web, which made a solid footing for the six hundred millions of the foot-soldiery. Phæton had an equally formidable force of gnat-riders, slingers from the milky way, cloud-centaurs, etc.

Phaeton's defeat was decisive; the clouds were even tinged with blood, and some drops fell to the earth, — which may account, Lucian thinks, for the shower of blood which Homer says Jupiter rained down at Sarpedon's death. Two trophies of victory were erected, — one on the cobweb, and the other on the clouds. But they were too soon in their rejoicing. While they were thus dispersed and unprepared, the cloud-centaurs came up, headed by Sagittarius from the zodiac. It was a terrific sight, — these half-men, half-horse creatures; the human part as large as the upper half of the Colossus at Rhodes, and the horse-half as large as a ship, and their number so prodigious that the narrator declines to state it *lest he should not be believed !* The narrator and his companions are taken prisoners and carried to the sun. Endymion was besieged in his capital, and a great wall built up to deprive him of the light. He is brought to terms, and peace is happily concluded. The Selenites do not die, but vanish like smoke into the air. They snuff up the effluvia of what they roast, instead of eating the meat itself; and for drink they squeeze moisture out of the air. They esteem a bald head a beauty, while on the comets curly hair is the fashion. Their eyes they can take out at pleasure and put them in their pockets. In the king's palace is a wonderful looking-glass, and any one who looks into it can see all that is happening on the earth. "If any one disbelieves this," adds the author, "if he ever goes thither he may convince himself with his own eyes that the whole is true."

The travellers have many other adventures in the celestial regions, but are infinitely rejoiced at last to find themselves sailing again on their own watery element. But a great whale, three hundred miles long, cáme towards them and swallowed ship and all at one gulp. They entered a cavity of vast extent, where were bones, cargoes of ships, sails, anchors, and a small island with trees and hills, — some floating island which the monster had swallowed. In the trees were various birds, and the dejected crew made themselves as comfortable as they could. They find in the interior a temple dedicated to Neptune, and a man and a boy who had been enclosed, also, in that living, moving tomb. The man tells his story: he had been there twenty-seven years, and could be very comfortable were it not for the horrid monsters of all sorts that inhabited the interior of their abode, and were divided into different races which were at war with one another. The old man, living among the Psettopydes, or lobster-footed race, remarkable for their swiftness, paid them an annual tribute of five hundred oysters. As their only weapons were fish-bones, it was determined to fight them at once. Half the crew were placed in ambush, and fell upon the rear of the advancing host, who were defeated with great slaughter, while only one of the crew was killed. Fresh enemies came up, but were sent packing, and driven out of the whale's jaws into the sea.

After staying a year and eight months in the whale's belly, the unlucky travellers began to contrive some way of exit.  After digging till they were tired, they concluded to set fire to the forests, beginning at the extremity near his tail.  After eleven days the fire began to tell on the monster, and his strength declined, so that they were able to prop his mouth open with an immense beam, haul out their vessel, and put to sea again.  They now sailed through seas of milk, got frozen up, saw men walking on the sea, who were like themselves in every respect except that they had cork feet.  Then our travellers came to the Islands of the Blessed; fragrant breezes of the lily, violet, and vine were wafted toward them, enchanting zephyrs whispered around, and harmonious strains resounded from the groves; they heard also singing, and the music of instruments.  Upon going ashore, they found that Rhadamanthus the Cretan was the sovereign.  The city was of gold, surrounded by walls of emeralds; the pavement was of ivory, the houses of beryl, and the altars of amethyst.  Round the city flowed a stream of fragrant oil-of-roses; the baths were of crystal, and filled with warm dew.  The inhabitants had no bodies of flesh and bone, but were souls with a semblance of body wrapped about them, — upright shadows, as it were, which, instead of being black, had the natural color of bodies, and looked so natural that one had to touch them to be convinced that they were not corporeal forms.  They never grew old, and enjoyed a perpetual

4

spring. Their drinking-glasses bloomed on trees of transparent glass, and flocks of nightingales brought chaplets and dropped them on their heads. At the table songs and poems were chanted, and before they sat down they drank at the fountains of mirth and laughter. The Epicureans were here held in highest esteem; the Stoics were not present, being still engaged in climbing their hill of virtue; the Academics stood hesitating, and doubting whether to enter or not. The narrator found there the old heroes; and when he left the island, Ulysses drew him aside and gave him a letter to Calypso, which Penelope was to know nothing about. The travellers now passed some islands which were as offensive as the others were delightful, and at last came to the land of dreams, where they tarried thirty days. Calypso entertained them magnificently on her island, and put several questions to them in regard to Penelope, — how she looked, and whether she was really such a model of virtue as Ulysses had boasted. After leaving Calypso they sailed past a wonderful halcyon's nest, and strange prodigies happened: the goose on their prow began to cackle, the steersman's bald pate became covered with fine hair, and the masts began to sprout out with figs and clusters of grapes. Other wonderful adventures are related in the soberest way as facts, until the navigators return to their native land.

Here are Rabelais, Munchausen, and Gulliver combined.

Great, indeed, must have been the demoralization of the popular belief in polytheism for Lucian to have written his "Council of the Gods." The question under consideration among the Deities is the abuses that have crept into their general assembly, and the undue increase in the number of those who occupy celestial seats. Jupiter calls a council to debate upon the matter, and opens the meeting thus:

"Ye Gods! stop this grumbling between your teeth, this whispering in corners, about so many who are unworthy of the honor of sitting down at table. Let every one speak his mind freely. Mercury, perform your office.

*Mercury.* Ho! Silence! Every deity of full age is privileged to speak.

*Momus.* I say it is abominable that so many, not content with being made gods out of men, imagine that their new dignity gives them a right to put their train of followers into the same class with us, to bring their pot-companions with them into heaven, and get them enrolled in our register by stealth; so that these upstarts and intruders now partake in all the gifts and sacrifices, and receive an equal portion with us, though they never once think of paying their protection fees.

*Jupiter.* Speak with more directness, Momus, and give us the names of those you have reference to. Use the frankness that you plume yourself so much upon."

Momus does speak frankly about Bacchus and his drunken troop of followers; Silenus and Pan, — the one an old bald-pate with a flat nose, and generally riding on an ass, except when he is sc drunk that he cannot hold on; and the other with horns and beard and goat's feet. He also has something to say against Jupiter himself, who turned himself into so many forms and filled the assembly with such an illegitimate crowd,— declaring that the gods often feared lest, in the course of his masquerading, he might sometime or other be seized as a bull and slaughtered, or fall into a goldsmith's hand and be melted up into a bracelet or ear-ring.

"And you Egyptian dog's face!" Momus continues, " how came you to think you may bark among the gods? And what means that pied bull of Memphis, with his oracles and prophets, — and the storks and apes and goats and other preposterous deities that have been foisted into heaven? And how you, Jupiter, can endure to have a pair of ram's horns clapped on your head is past my comprehension.

*Jupiter.* It is really infamous! However, in most of these objects there lies at bottom a mystical meaning, which one who is not initiated should not presume to deride.

*Momus.* But, after all, we have no need of mysteries in order to know that gods are gods, and dog's heads dog's heads.

*Jupiter.* Let these matters alone, and proceed, if you have any more objections to offer."

Momus proceeds in the same vein, and finally reads the following decree, drawn up in due form:

"At a general council of the gods, beneath the auspices of Jupiter, under the presidency of Neptune, on the motion of Apollo, Momus the son of Night has drawn up this decree, to which Sleep has given his approval:

*Whereas*, a great number of foreigners, Greeks as well as Barbarians, have clandestinely got themselves enrolled in our register, and have so crowded heaven that our table is overstocked with a tumultuous rabble, and thence has ensued such a deficiency of nectar and ambrosia that we are obliged to pay twelve ounces of silver for a pint of nectar; And *whereas*, these intruders have insolently presumed to shove out the ancient and true deities from the first seats,—be it *Resolved* by this Council, that, on the next winter solstice, a general council shall be held, and a committee composed of seven of the gods shall be appointed, three of whom shall be taken from the old council under Saturn, and four elected from the twelve deities of Olympus, whereof Jupiter is to be one. The said committee shall first be required to take a solemn oath by Styx, and Mercury shall officially summon all who think that they have a right to assist in the divine councils, and they shall bring their sworn witnesses and records before the said committee, and shall be either declared true gods or sent back to their family vaults; and if any of those rejected shall ever again dare to look into or set foot in heaven, they shall be hurled down to Tartarus. And further be it ordained, that every deity shall mind his own business, and neither Minerva meddle with healing, nor Esculapius with fortune-telling; and let Apollo select one profession, and be either a fortune-teller, a fiddler, or a physician; and furthermore, let the altars, images, and temples of the rejected be demolished. Whoever disobeys this decree, or refuses to appear before the committee, shall be condemned for contumacy without further process. Such is our decree.

*Jupiter.* It could not be better. So many as are in

favor of it will hold up their hands. Or, rather, let it be ratified without any show of hands; for there are too many that will not vote the right way, for very good reasons of their own. Now, Gods, you may go. But when Mercury summons you, let every one bring his patent of godship, the name of his father and mother, and how he came to be a god, and of what stock he is. If any one cannot produce these legal documents, no matter how magnificent a temple he may have on earth, the committee will pay no regard to it."

How like a modern document this paper sounds, though written in the second century; and what a satire upon the polytheism of the ancient world, crumbling to pieces, while out of its débris was springing up a purer and more universal faith!

Another popular superstition that Lucian unmasked with all his powers of biting drollery was the belief in ghosts, spirits, and demonic possessions. From the many passages that relate to this recurring theme, and that give us the very body and pressure of this period of miracles and spiritual wonders, one transcription will suffice:

" While we were thus conversing, in came Arignotus the Pythogorean, of a grave and venerable aspect, renowned for his wisdom, and by many styled the holy Arignotus. I felt cheered to see him, for I thought he would stop the mouths of these miracle-mongers. He began by asking, 'Have you not been philosophizing?' Said Dinomachus, 'I have been trying to convince this unbelieving man that there are such things as ghosts and spectres, and that the souls of the dead roam about the earth and become visible when they please.' 'Perhaps,' replied Arignotus, 'it is his opinion that the souls only of those who have died a violent death wander to and fro. If this is his belief, he may not be greatly in the wrong.' 'No, by Jove!' cried Dinomachus, 'he denies everything of the kind, absolutely and entirely, and thinks that it is utterly impossible.' 'How!' said Arignotus, looking sternly at me; 'you deny the reality of what the whole human race bears witness to?' 'The accusation of unbelief justifies me,' I replied; 'I do not believe, because I am the only one who does not see anything of the kind. Had I seen, I should doubtless believe as well as you.' 'If you should ever go to Corinth,' said Arignotus, 'ask for the house of Eubatides; and when you go in, tell the porter you would like to see the place from which Arignotus expelled the evil spirit.' 'Tell us about it, Arignotus.' 'Well,' replied he, 'whoever entered the house was sure to be frightened by a horrid apparition. The house became uninhabited and almost fell to ruin. I resolved to stay there one night, in spite of all entreaties to the contrary. A rough and shaggy demon appeared, turning himself into a dog, then a bull, and then a lion; but I made use of most fearful imprecations and incantations in the Egyptian tongue, and the spectre vanished. I marked the spot where it disappeared, and ordering the ground to be dug up we found there a skeleton. We buried it with proper sacred rites, and no ghost has ever been seen there since.'"

But this was not just the evidence that would satisfy Lucian, however satisfactory it may have been to Arignotus himself.

The philosophers of the time are as little spared by the satirist as are the devotees of superstition. He gives the history of one Peregrinus, who finally burned himself alive. On the road home from the spectacle, Lucian meets several persons hurrying along, who are too late to witness it. He gravely tells some of the gaping simpletons who question him about the event, that as soon as Peregrinus jumped into the flames the earth began to quake, and a vulture flew up to heaven and uttered these words: "Soaring above the earth, I ascend to Olympus." Shuddering with awe, the poor people breathe a prayer to the new demi-god, and ask whether the vulture flew toward the east or toward the west. Afterward, he hears an old man recounting in the public market-place how he himself had seen, but a few moments before, the burnt philosopher walking in the sacred grove in white raiment and with an olive wreath on his brow; and that he had beheld the vulture with his own eyes fly up from the fire. "What miraculous things will hereafter be related of this man!" says Lucian.

This Peregrinus, changing from one philosophical sect to another, at last joins the sect of Christians, and is thrown into prison. In his wretchedness, his fellow-believers come from far distant cities to be his advocates, and to assist and comfort him,—for these people, in all such cases, are inconceivably alert and active, sparing neither trouble nor expense. Large presents were made to Peregrinus; "for these poor people," he says, "have taken it into their heads that they shall be immortal, both body and soul, and live to all eternity; and so they despise death, and even run into his clutches. Besides, their law-giver taught them that they were all brothers after they had once renounced the Grecian deities, bent the knee to the great Sophist, and lived in obedience to his laws. All things else they look upon as worthless and vain; and whenever any cunning impostor applies to them, who understands the proper trick, he finds it an easy matter to lead these simple people by the nose, and very soon to become rich at their expense."

What an involuntary testimony is here borne to the character of those early Christians, — their simplicity, their faith, their mutual love, and their heroic contempt of danger and of death! Could not the enlightened speculator on human nature and human affairs discern this seemingly feeble germ? His work was to topple down the old temples, to cover the remnants of old superstitions with laughter and contempt, and bury out of sight the hideous forms of licentious and unreasoning idolatry. His sweeping scythe could not discriminate, and in its broad sweep cut down thistle, white-weed, and clover alike; but thereby free space and air were given for the tender germs of a purer faith to grow up, to be for long ages the sustenance of humanity.

Thus in Lucian's page there pass before us the scenes of that long-vanished age, — the shifting scenes of kings and beggars, parasites and slaves; wealthy blockheads displaying affectedly the purple borders of their garments, spreading their fingers that their rings may be seen, and saluting by proxy their acquaintances in the street; people besieging the door of their patrons before it is light; men of reverend years hanging about the rich man's table; philosophers with their long beards and mantles mingling among the attendants and fawning sycophants of the great, preaching contempt of riches and yet selling their wares to the highest bidders; wealthy people, still so enamoured of their preposterous vanities as to order in their wills that their best valuables should be burned on their funeral piles, and that their slaves should keep perpetual watch at their sepulchres and decorate their tombs with flowers; believers in spirit communications and rappings, in ghosts, in auguries, in oracles and divinations, so that sometimes we seem to be reading some "Banner of Light," of the present day.

"You know how much I loved my dear, departed wife," says one. "I have shown it by burning with her all her jewels and the dress she most delighted in. Seven days after her death I was lying on this couch, trying to console myself, and reading Plato on the immortality of the soul. All at once I beheld my Demeneta sitting where that boy now is. (Here he pointed to his youngest son, who had begun to turn pale at his father's recital,

and was now quite ghastly.)   I embraced her, and she
wept like a child.   She complained that I, who used to
do everything to please her, had neglected to burn with
her one of her golden sandals.   She said that it had fallen
down behind a clothes-chest, — that was the reason I
could not find it.   My little dog began now to bark, and
she immediately vanished.   The sandal was afterward
found behind the clothes-chest, and on the following day
it was burned."

Is it of the second or the nineteenth century that
we are reading in this recital?

But we must bid farewell to this more than
ghostly re-appearance of the vanished century.
As a picture of the life and manners of a great
part of the civilized world in a peroid of decay-
ing beliefs and crumbling forms of philosophy
and religion, — a period of external peace but of
inward corruption; a period when all the vices,
the licentious superstitions, the sensual extrava-
gances, the idolatries, the humbugs, the seething
and fermenting pretentions and lies of long ages
of delusion met in the world's great capital and
mingled in one great maelstrom, whose fierce
whirl was felt to the remotest lands, — as a picture of this, as a culminating expression of the
life of polytheistic Greece and Rome, from which
all earnest belief had forever fled, — as one of the
heralds of a higher and a fairer doctrine of God,
of duty, and of immortality, this writer is worthy
of our passing attention.   But it is a hollow laugh
that echoes mournfully through these desolate

vaults.   We ask for something more,— something
that shall feed our souls with faith and love and
reverence; something that shall lift us into a
more holy sphere and help us to believe, to be
strong, and to hope, while the years flit by as a
passing dream, and the centuries are folded up as
a written scroll.

# III.

## A SCEPTIC IN THE EIGHTEENTH CENTURY.

EDGAR QUINET calls the eighteenth century "the migration of the modern world from one form of society into another," and speaks of Voltaire as "the spiritual director of this epoch," as seated upon that spiritual throne which was held by the Papacy in the Middle Age.

Voltaire's real name was François Marie Arouet. Born in 1694, he was early sent to a Jesuit college, frequented by the sons of the *haute noblesse*. He received the nickname among his mates of the "little wilful," and was a prodigy of vivacious quick-wittedness, mischief, and boyish audacity. "Keep out of the way!" the precocious sceptic as well as wit said to one of his comrades who intercepted the heat of the fireplace, — "keep out of the way, or I 'll send you to Pluto's realms." "Why not say hell? That 's warmer yet," said his comrade. "How do you know that?" rejoined Voltaire; "there 's no better warrant for the one than for the other." At another time, when one said to him that "he was too wicked ever to go to heaven," he replied, "Heaven! heaven! that 's nothing but a great dormitory for the world."

To sneer at religion among these aristocratic youths was the mark of a high spirit. The memoirs of that time reveal a fearful state of corruption in the entire social atmosphere. The shameful profligacy of the court was only equalled by its superstitious formality, and by the austere bigotry of devotees, who compounded with the Celestial Powers for their sins by the orthodoxy of their creed, and by the fierceness of their zeal against all forms of heresy. When Voltaire was only twelve years old, one of his reverend tutors prophesied that he would become the "Corypheus of Deism in France." But, as Lord Brougham well says, "Whoever doubted the real presence, or questioned the power of absolution, was at once set down for an infidel in those times;" and a trifle of wit mingled with the argument would readily brand one as a blasphemer. In Voltaire's case, neither the wit nor the will was wanting. In one respect, the youth of the juvenile scapegrace was not the father of the man; for in his manhood he was prudent in money matters, and accumulated an immense fortune, so that he became the creditor of many a nobleman, and was noted for his shrewdness and his sharp eye to the main chance. In his youthful days he had occasion to make a visit to a money-lender; and he gives the following narration of his experience:

"I found on the usurer's table two crucifixes, and I asked him whether they had been left to pawn. He said no; but that he never made any bargain without having those crucifixes near. I said that I thought one would do, and my advice was to place that one between two thieves. He said I was an impious fellow, and he would not loan me a cent; but he did let me have money at twenty per cent interest, on security worth five times the sum, — deducting the interest in advance, and finally decamping with my securities in his pocket."

It was, indeed, a horrible religious atmosphere for a young man to breathe, not too well endowed with reverence and spiritual insight. Religion was a part of the State machinery, and only as it persecuted heretics did it show signs of being alive. To be a Protestant was to be an outlaw; to be a Papist was to possess the right of trampling upon every individual conviction and all venerable and instinctive moralities. No period of the world presents a more gruesome and loathsome spectacle of religious immorality and of immoral religion. The court was austerely devout; polite society was ostentatiously vicious, and bigotedly unbigoted in its licentiousness and unbelief. The court formed itself upon Madame de Maintenon, and "good society" upon Ninon de l'Enclos. Madame endeavored to bribe the wonderful coquette to become a *devotee;* but she replied that she had no need either of a fortune or a mask.

To Ninon, Voltaire was early introduced by his godfather, the Abbé Châteauneuf, as a desirable acquaintance. She was then eighty years old; and when she died she left to Voltaire, by will, two thousand francs for the purchase of books. One of his first purchases from this fund was Bayle's "Philosophical Dictionary," — the great mine from which the doubters of the eighteenth century forged their pointed shafts of criticism and raillery.

Being suspected of having written a satire which seemed to cast some severe reflections upon the memory of Louis XIV., Voltaire was sent to the Bastile when twenty-two years of age, and again, a few years afterward, for some personal quarrel with a courtier who was entirely in the wrong. In the Bastile he wrote the "Henriade," whose hero was the great advocate of religious toleration, and who was as good at a *bon mot* in its behalf as Voltaire himself. When set free from the Bastile by the regent, Philip of Orleans, the poet went to the Palais Royal to pay his respects to his patron, and was kept waiting in the antechamber longer than suited his impatient spirit. While waiting, a terrible thunder-storm broke over their heads; and the fuming youth exclaimed in the hearing of those about him, "Things could n't go on worse if they were managed up above there by a regency." On presenting him, the Marquis de Nocé reported the speech, saying, "Monseigneur, this is the young Arouet whom you have just taken out of the Bastile, and whom you will do well to send back again immediately." The regent, laughing, offered Voltaire a pension. His response to this offer was, "I thank his Royal

Highness for wishing to provide for my food; but I humbly entreat that he will not be very anxious to provide for my lodging."

When ordered to leave Paris, on his release from his second imprisonment in the Bastile, Voltaire went to England; and here was, undoubtedly, the turning-point of his entire future career. English freedom and English thought were just beginning to influence the thinking minds of his countrymen. French literature and French science were almost extinguished under the combined influences of arbitrary power and priestly intolerance. Books were burned and authors imprisoned at the pleasure of a bigoted ecclesiasticism and a superstitious civil rule; and when educated men became acquainted with the literature and laws of England, the contrast of its freedom in thought, freedom in worship, its government of constitutional law and guaranteed rights, with their helpless subjection to absolute and priestly rule, awakened the deepest desire to study yet more intimately English literature, English science, and English political institutions.

Into the midst of these institutions, this comparatively wonderful and admirable freedom of life and thought, Voltaire was thrown by the operation of arbitrary power. He was brought under such influences as that of Newton in physical science, of Locke in mental philosophy, of Shakspeare in poetry, of Shaftesbury and the English Deists in religion. Cousin says, "Before Voltaire knew

5

England he was not Voltaire; and the eighteenth century was yet looking for its king." Everywhere in his writings he dwells with enthusiasm on the popular freedom of England, on its steady maintenance of human rights against oppressors in Church and State. "How I love," he cries out, " the English boldness! How I love those who speak out what they think!" This was not possible in France, where, as Buckle says, "if a list were drawn up of all the literary men who wrote during the seventy years succeeding the death of Louis XIV., it would be found that at least nine out of every ten had suffered some grievous injury from the government, and that a majority of them had been actually thrown into prison. Among those authors who were punished, I find the name of nearly every Frenchman whose writings have survived the age in which they were produced."

Voltaire thoroughly learns in England how to say what he thinks. But if he likes the English freedom, he dislikes the English gloom of temperament, which he attributes to the fogginess of the climate and the prevalence of the east wind. He meets some gentlemen who were in admirable spirits the day before, but who now are all gloomy and depressed. He ventures to ask one what is the matter, and gets for a reply that the wind is east. "At that instant, a gentleman comes in and says, with unconcern, that Molly's lover had found her dead, with a bloody razor by her side. No one raised an eyebrow at the news, one of the friends only asking, 'What became of the lover?' 'Oh,' coldly replied one of the company, 'he afterward purchased the razor.' I could not, on my part, refrain from inquiring into the cause of the frightful catastrophe ; and they simply replied, 'The wind was east.' And a famous physician afterward told me that when Charles I. was beheaded and James II. dethroned, the wind was east." M. Taine has thoroughly worked up this east wind in his criticism of English literature.

When Voltaire returned to France and attempted to publish a book on England, he was again sent to the Bastile. Thus he was made to feel the annoyances of petty despotism and ecclesiastical hate. They are the objects of his ever-bubbling denunciation; but they do not wholly pervert his judgment. When some one asserted that the Jesuits had a settled design to corrupt the morals of mankind, he maintained that "no sect and no society ever had, or ever could have, such a design." From first to last, he protested against what Bunsen called "a theological system which had renounced both reason and science." He protested in bitter words and with scornful laughter against the hollow mockeries of a superstition which called itself by the sacred name of Christ, and stood in the way of all progress in knowledge, all real faith in God, and in the universe as the creation of his universal love.

Voltaire always theoretically protested against atheism. "There is no religion," he says, " in which we do not find a supreme God over all; and there is no one which was not originally established in order to make men less vicious." While the other writers of the Encyclopædia were pronounced atheists and materialists, calling virtue "a wisely understood selfishness," religion "a gaseous effusion of the brain," and God "a creation of superstition and fear," Voltaire and Rousseau protested against these extremes, and became the butt of ridicule among their compeers. Grimm says sneeringly of the former, "The patriarch can't get rid of his remunerating avenger."

In 1752 Voltaire began the "Dictionnaire Philosophique." The idea was first broached at one of King Frederick's philosophic suppers. But of all men Voltaire least deserves the title of a philosopher; and his treatment of great topics, not methodically, but alphabetically, well typifies the prevailing want of all method in thought, and the overthrow of what may be called true philosophic thinking. But the Dictionary enabled him to treat of such subjects as he pleased, in the manner he pleased. Wherever the opportunity offers, he improves it to probe superstitions, stab ecclesiastical nonsense, and ridicule received dogmas. Thus, under the title "Abbé," he writes: —

"I hear the abbés of Italy, Germany, Flanders, Burgundy, saying: ' Why should not we accumulate riches and honors? Why should not we be princes like the bishops? They were originally poor as we; they have become rich and exalted; one of them has become superior to kings: let us imitate them as well as we can.' You are right, gentlemen. Seize upon the earth: it belongs to the strong or the able, who may take possession of it. You have made good use of the times of ignorance, of superstition, of folly, to despoil us of our inheritance and to trample us under your feet, and fatten yourselves on the substance of the wretched. Tremble lest the day of reason shall come!"

He ends his article on "Democracy" by saying:

"Every day the question is asked whether a republican government be preferable to that of a king. The discussion always ends by agreeing that it is a very difficult thing to govern men. The Jews had God himself for a master, and see what has happened to them: they have been almost always conquered and enslaved; and do you not think that to-day they cut a very fine figure?"

Again, under "Abraham," he writes: —

"Certainly, if one looks upon this account as natural, he must have an understanding very different from what we have to-day, or he must consider each detail as miraculous, or believe that the whole is an allegory; but whatever theory is adopted, it is very embarrassing."

Among the works of Voltaire bearing directly upon religion is a collection of sermons and homilies, supposed to have been delivered at different places and times by persons of various nations and creeds. He can thus view the phases of Christian belief and practice from each religion as a central point. The first sermon is delivered to an assembly of fifty, who meet on Sunday, have prayers and a sermon, then dine together, and take up a collection for the poor. Each member is president in turn, and conducts the religious services. The first sermon begins thus: —

" My brothers, religion is the secret voice of God which speaks to all men. It ought to unite them together, and not to divide them. Every religion, therefore, which belongs exclusively to one nation must be false. Religion ought to be universal, like morality; and every religion which offends the moral law must surely be false."

Then the morality of the Scriptures is scrutinized, as follows: —

" You know, brethren, what horror has seized upon us when we have read together the Hebrew books, and our attention has been called to the violations of purity, good faith, justice, charity, and universal reason, which are not only there, but there in the name of God."

The examples of such violations are then specified in detail, and the discourse closes with the prayer that men may become "more truly religious, adorers of the one God of justice and love, and less the victims of ignorance and superstition."

Another sermon is by a Jewish rabbi in Smyrna, who takes for his theme the horrible executions made by the savages of Lisbon, called an *auto-da-fé*, or "act of faith," wherein two Mohammedans and thirty-seven Jews were burned to death.

Another takes for its theme God and man: —

" They say that God's justice is not our justice. They might as well say that twice two is four is not the same truth to God and man. There are not two different kinds of truth. We can comprehend God's justice only by the idea we have of justice in ourselves. God, as an infinite being, must be infinitely just."

In another discourse, it is maintained —

" that no prophet or leader ever gained disciples by preaching vice or crime. Jesus preached a universal morality, — love to God and love to man. He never intended to found this Christianity, which, as it has existed since the time of Constantine, has been further removed from Jesus than from Zoroaster or Brahma. Jesus has been made the pretext for our fantastic doctrines, our persecutions, our crimes against religion; but he was not their author. The horrible calamities with which Christianity has inundated countries where it has been introduced afflict me, and make me shed tears; and I despise that heart of ice which is not moved when it considers the religious troubles which have agitated England, Ireland, and Scotland."

In another place he thus apostrophizes: —

"God of justice and of peace! let us expiate by toleration the crimes which an execrable intolerance has caused us to commit. Come to my house rational Socinian, friendly Quaker, strict Lutheran, gloomy Presbyterian, indifferent Episcopalian, Mennonite, Millenarian, Methodist, Pietist, — you, too, mad Papal slave, provided you have no hidden poniard! — let us bow together before the Supreme Being, and thank him for having given us reason to know him and hearts to love him; let us eat joyfully together after giving him thanks."

We can but be sorry for that suggestion of the possible dagger hidden under the robe of the Catholic brother, and doubt if Voltaire had arrived at perfect toleration.

As an historical writer, Voltaire was in advance of his age. His speculative view, not narrowed by partiality for church or sect, led him to write, not so much the history of dynasties and special institutions, as to unfold the great interests of humanity and its advance from barbarism to civilization. Where Bossuet saw only one little stream of development through ecclesiastical channels, Voltaire saw the great outspread ocean, into which ran all the rivers from mountain and plain. The principles of historical criticism he carried out consistently, applying them to the Jewish as well as to Greek and Roman narratives: —

"These books," he says, "are not judges in their own cause. I do not believe Livy when he tells us that Romulus was son of the god Mars. I do not believe the early English authors when they say that Vortiger was a sorcerer. I do not believe the old historians of the Franks when they refer their origin to Francus, the son of Hector. And I ought not to believe the Jews on their own testimony alone, when they relate extraordinary events."

The spirit of Voltaire, mocking, irreverent, bitter, and relentless, found an ample field in which to disport itself. He early learned to set little value upon the hard names by which he was called.

He had heard Lord Shaftesbury everywhere denounced by Roman Catholic writers as an atheist,
yet Lord Shaftesbury maintained that "perfection
of virtue was owing to a belief in God." He had
heard Jansenists denounce Jesuits, and Jesuits
accuse Jansenists as godless. Even pure and devout men like Malebranche, Pascal, and Arnauld
did not escape. Those who spoke or wrote against
the follies of the *convulsionnaire* mania, that seized
entire districts, were stigmatized as atheists; and
it was gravely charged against an advocate of the
newly introduced discovery of inoculation for small-
pox, that he was "an atheist infected by the follies of the English." He heard Bayle universally
spoken of as an atheist, because he maintained as a
theoretical speculation that a community of atheists might still be held together by moral and social bonds,—a proposition which Mill and many
others to-day have advanced with impunity. He
saw that it was called atheism merely to question
the sufficiency of any alleged proof of God's existence, or of any propositions dependent thereon.

But Voltaire had his little *revanche,* when the
good Dr. Wolfius, an innocent soul and a worthy
man, ventured to praise the morality of the Chi-
nese, whom the Jesuit missionaries had called a
nation of atheists, and was, in consequence, overwhelmed with accusations of atheism. Now, when
extreme words are thus indiscriminately used,
it shows that they have lost their meaning, have
become emptied of their real contents. He who

truly believes in God shrinks from saying that any one is an atheist; but he in whose inmost soul the word θεός stands for little of moment will easily put the privative letter before the word, and brandish it about as lustily as an athlete his Indian club. In one of his prefaces, Voltaire says that the "odious and ridiculous practice of accusing as atheists all who are not exactly of the same sentiments with us, has contributed more than any other cause whatever to render controversy contemptible to all Europe."

Voltaire especially gloried in being a poet, — one of the crowned kings of verse. Whatever the great bards had done, he would do also; and he essays the construction of an epic which should be the Iliad of the French nation. He writes "La Henriade." To us of to-day, Voltaire and poetry seem incongruous enough. The poem, however, on its publication was received with an immense *furor* of praise; but it requires now a telescopic lens of great magnifying power to bring it fairly into view. Purely local in its subject, unfortunate in taking for that subject the civil war in the time of Henry IV. of France, it contains the most absurd allegorical machinery, and is true neither to ideal demands nor to historic fact. But the real Voltaire, in the midst of extravagant exaggerations and conventional imitations, shows himself in his description of the massacre of St. Bartholomew, at the anniversary of which he was said always to have been feverishly excited; and not less he shows himself in his description of the festival of toleration celebrated in the heavenly regions.[1]

To Voltaire belongs the credit of widening the range of tragic themes by stepping beyond the charmed circle of classic subjects, and seizing upon material drawn from China, from Babylon, from Mecca, from Peru, and from French historical events. He sought for something to move the fancy, something which would carry in itself a striking effect upon the imagination. He believed in declamation, in phrases, and in melodramatic scenes, and his style imposes upon the imagination rather than meets its wants. During his residence in England, he was deeply impressed by the drama of Shakspeare; but he never did, and

---

[1] The measureless self-conceit and vanity of the man, and his inability to estimate epic poetry, are to be seen in some verses which he addressed to Madame ———— " On the Epic Poets," of which a literal translation is as follows : " Full of beauties and defects, old Homer has my respect. He is, like all heroes, a great gossip, but sublime. Virgil gives more ornament to his matter, has more skill, and as much harmony ; but he exhausts himself with Dido, and makes a failure of Lavinia. False brilliants and too much magic put Tasso a notch lower ; but what will one not endure for Armida and Hermione? Milton, more sublime than they all, has less pleasing beauties ; he seems to sing for mad men, angels, and devils. After Milton, after Tasso, it would be a little too much to speak of myself ; and I shall wait until after my death to learn what place belongs to *me*." But the old wit, even after he was fourscore, could turn a handsome compliment ; and he does it now, closing his verses on the epic poets as follows : " You, Madame, have so much wit, so much grace, and so much sweetness, if my place is in your heart, it is the first place in the world." We may add that it is well for him that his ambition was so easily satisfied.

never could, comprehend the real genius of the great dramatist, whose plays he called *monstrous farces, misnamed tragedies!* He could not help discerning the impressiveness of individual scenes, but he had no idea of the dramatic art as a national development. With him, the spectacle and the declamation were all. He says:—

"It is far more difficult to write well than to put upon the stage ghosts, assassins, rakes, gibbets, and witches. Works in verse must depend upon particular beauties; and if Addison's 'Cato' is the masterpiece of English dramatic art, it owes its place to nothing but to these."

Yes; Addison's "Cato," absolutely correct in the unities, decorous and stately in language, exceedingly well-phrased, euphonious, and eloquent, is simply the antipodes to Shakspeare in all that concerns the real essence of dramatic art. Hence it is, no doubt, genuine praise that Voltaire bestows upon it. Shakspeare is only a barbarian and a hangman, who looks neither to style nor to conventional unities, nor to proprieties before the court and the nobility. Horrible, that his kings should use the language of the *canaille!* Horrible, that genuine emotion should be expressed in genuine words of ordinary life! Horrible, that men and women should do such a vulgar thing as die in the presence of princes, and that princes and kings should be simple, ordinary men!

It is only natural that Voltaire should fail to detect the purely human character of Shakspeare's dramas. Quick he was to feel deeply and declaim eloquently against injustice and wrong; but it was only *priestly* injustice and *ecclesiastical* wrong that filled him thus with bitterness, and thrilled through every fibre of his being. The worth of man as man, and the dreams of universal humanity never dawned upon Voltaire, so versatile, so acute, so inimical to corruptions, abuses, and shams. He was a courtier and a sycophant. He had no be- lief in the people, but an unlimited faith in the regeneration of the world by philosophic kings. He had a profound contempt for what was purely natural, simple, unostentatious, and genuine; and how could he discern the nice humanities of Shak- speare's genius, the delicate forms throbbing with their inner life, and true to the faintest breath of natural passion and imaginative love!

Voltaire claims to have attained that quality which was indispensable, — simplicity; and he condescendingly exhorts English poets to soften the rude manners of their savage Melpomene, and labor for the approval of all times and all ages. He would have them introduce a happy simpli- city into their plays, so tainted with horrors, gib- bets, and slaughter; to put into them more truth and more noble images. A strange spectacle,— Voltaire finding fault with Shakspeare for his want of noble images, true simplicity, and tenderness in love! We are not surprised, therefore, that he calls Shakspeare's "Hamlet" "a gross and barbar- ous play, which would not be endured by the vilest populace of France or Italy." His standard of taste was wholly conventional. To some one, speaking of the natural force of that expression in Shakspeare to indicate the undisturbed silence of the watch, — "not a mouse stirring," — he replied: "Yes, that is the way a soldier on guard would speak; but that is not the way to express one's self on the stage in the presence of the most noble ladies of the nation, who express themselves in noble style, and before whom noble expressions ought also to be used."

What can we expect from such a point of view as this? Surely, nothing more than we find, — stiff formality, cold elegance, attention to fine speeches rather than dramatic unfoldings of character; striking points in situation instead of fidelity to nature; effective declamation, not language springing from natural feeling and the necessities of the situation, — in a word, a drama classical in form, correct in style, and, above all, pre-eminently genteel and courtly in air, conforming to the unities, and violating none of the received critical dogmas. Such was the drama of Voltaire, who slavishly followed precedent here if nowhere else in life.

Sharp in intellect, indefatigable in industry, with a vast memory and an ever-ready wit, Voltaire composed a whole library of books, verses, epics, plays, criticisms, letters, biographies, tales, and histories, each related to the times, and each the embodiment of his own personality in some promi-

nent phase of its development. Principles he had
none; his own individual prejudices and likings
were his only rules. He obeyed the dominant
impulse of the moment, and without real passion
was the most passionate of men. He did not belong to the new age: he was the avenging Nemesis
of the old, and never shook off its poisonous folds.

The strenuous labors of Voltaire for those condemned and oppressed by the iniquitous laws, gave
him his great European reputation. This became
notoriety from the intercourse between Frederick
the Great and the renowned poet-philosopher, —
first by that friendship which received the com-
moner as an equal, and treated him as a brother
king; and then by that enmity which made Voltaire almost the central point of European gossip
in court and social circles. Frederick urged him
to come to Berlin in the following letter, blas-
phemous if it were not so fulsome and silly:

" There is a small company of persons who have set up
altars to the god whom they have not seen ; but you may
be sure that some heretics will set up altars to Baal if *our
god* does not show himself pretty soon. You will be received as the Virgil of this century, and the gentleman-in-
ordinary of Louis XV. will give way, if he pleases, to the,
great poet. Adieu. May the swift steeds of Achilles
bear you on, and the highways be made plain before you !
May the inns of Germany be changed into palaces to receive you ! May the winds of Æolus be shut up in their
caves, the rainy Orion disappear, and our pot-house
nymphs be transformed into goddesses, so that your

journey and reception may be worthy of the author of
'Henriade'!"

Here also is Voltaire's *jubilate* soon after his
arrival:—

"My marriage has taken place: will it be a happy one?
My heart beats violently at the altar. It is the first time
that a king has governed without women and priests."

When at one of the philosophic suppers the
opinion of the king was first asked, Fr,ederick
made no reply. "Why do you not respond?"
some one asked. "The king," said he, "is not I:
he is Voltaire. When I am at the head of a hundred thousand men, I am the king; but when I sup
with Voltaire, he is the king."

But after a while we hear a different tune.
The peace of the happy family is disturbed, and
Voltaire writes:—

"I must forget this three years' dream. I see very
well that the orange has been sucked, and all I can do
is to save the peel. I am going to make for my own instruction a little dictionary of kingly dialect. 'My friend'
means 'my slave.' 'My dear friend' means 'You are more
than indifferent to me.' 'Sup with me this evening' means
'I am going to make fun of you this evening.' But I am
very sorrowful and very ill; and to crown my misery, I
take supper with the king!"

It seems to have been a real matrimonial tiff,
and a case of incompatible tempers. Of course
a divorce is possible, and the great poet-philoso-

pher, under a feigned name, left Berlin secretly; but he was arrested and thrown into prison on the charge of stealing a manuscript of the great Frederick's poems.

When he finally retired to Ferney, in Switzerland, Voltaire was more than sixty years old, having in the mean time accumulated a large fortune and become the central object of friends and foes. To receive homage was the claim of this intellectual king,— homage being as necessary to him as to any earthly potentate. The place fixed upon for his abode bordered upon four different countries, and he had now throngs of worshippers and multitudes of readers. With indefatigable industry he writes epistles, pamphlets, poems, flying leaves of all sorts, to amuse and interest an applauding, a horror-stricken, a distracted Europe hurrying to its judgment-day. He is absolutely without any of the ordinary and accepted reverences, fears, respects, or restraints; a devastating fire seems to have swept over and through his soul. But ecclesiastical abuses and intolerant cruelty touch a chord in him that never ceases to vibrate and send forth notes of warning and protest. He says what he likes, and does what a passing caprice dictates. A church on his grounds intercepts a fine view: he pulls it down and builds another, over whose portals is the inscription in Latin, DEO EREXIT VOLTAIRE, — "Erected to God by Voltaire." He builds a watch manufactory and a theatre, drains marshes, assists the poor, buys

6

books and pictures, and proposes to partake of the communion like "any other Christian citizen." But the bishop puts an injunction on this by ordering that no priest shall receive Voltaire's confession or grant him absolution. Not to be balked thus, the cunning old head pretends to be on his death-bed, sends for a priest, from whom he receives absolution, and gets the fact duly attested by the public notary. In return, moreover, for a piece of profitable intercession, he receives the title "temporal father of the Capuchins of Gex," which he makes a matter of humorous boasting.

Voltaire's wit spares neither friend nor foe. A provincial advocate in an eloquent address saluting him as a light of the world, he called to his niece, Madame Denis, "Madame, bring here the snuffers!" When he is past eighty, an enthusiastic young Englishwoman visits him, and thus writes concerning her interview: —

"Never did the transports of Saint Theresa surpass those which I experienced at the sight of this great man. It seemed to me that I was in the presence of a god. My heart beat with violence as I entered the courtyard of this consecrated château. Voltaire soon came in, saying: 'Where is she? It is a soul that I am looking for.' I replied, 'This soul is all filled with you: if your books were all burned, they would be found in me.' 'Revised and corrected,' was his witty reply."

When taking leave, this devoted admirer asked a blessing from the object of her adoration. At first he seemed at a loss how to respond to the request, but finally said: "I cannot bless you with my fingers, like a priest. I would rather put my arms around your neck." And this was his benediction.

In his eighty-fifth year, when Voltaire went for the last time to Paris, February, 1778, he was asked the usual question at the customs-barrier, whether he had anything contraband among his luggage. "Gentlemen," he replied, "the only contraband article I have is myself." But this contraband received such an ovation as monarch or conqueror rarely receives. The streets, the academy, the theatre, all ages and conditions except the court and the clergy, vied in paying him homage. "Long live Voltaire, the persecuted of fifty years!" was the cry. It was his day of jubilant success, and that all-absorbing love of fame which he cherished seemed fully gratified. But let it be recorded to his credit that no "sweet voices" of the applauding thousands gave him so much delight as the reply of the woman, who, when asked who it was the crowd were shouting after, said: "Do you not know that he is the savior of Calas?"[1]

Overwhelmed by the excitement of his triumphal visit, — "stifled with roses," as he himself

[1] Jean Calas had been condemned at Toulouse, and broken on the wheel, for a crime of which he was innocent, and his family had been driven from the country. Through Voltaire's generous exertions and untiring zeal, the sentence was annulled and the family of Calas partially indemnified.

expresses it,—Voltaire died in Paris in 1778. In 1791 his coffin was borne to the Pantheon, and deposited between that of Descartes and of Mirabeau,—"an apotheosis," says Lamartine, in his rhetorical phrase, of "intelligence entering in triumph over the ruins of prejudice into the city of Louis XIV."

But what of Voltaire's work? Quinet compares this with that of the angel of wrath pouring out upon the condemned Cities of the Plain sulphur and bitumen in the midst of the howling tempest: "So the spirit of Voltaire walked over the face of the divine city, and poured out gall, irony, and ashes. His work was not that of a private individual, but of an instrument of the vengeance of God." There was surely scope enough for any well-tempered instrument of this sort. As late as the year 1763 a young man was sentenced to the torture of the rack, to have his tongue torn out, and then to be beheaded. For what? For insulting a crucifix placed upon a bridge! In 1762 a Protestant father and mother were condemned to death on the charge of having killed their own daughter, who escaped from a convent and was found drowned in a well. At about the same time, five young men died on the scaffold for not taking off their hats when they saw a priestly procession pass along at a distance of thirty paces. Well may Voltaire say, in a letter to the Archduchess Louisa, "Religion among us is preached by executioners." Is it strange that Voltaire retaliated in the same spirit? Enfantin has rightly characterized Voltaire as doing his work in the spirit of an executioner, because "he struck without sympathy for his victims." Yes, it was God's century of judgment and destruction; and Voltaire was its chief apostle.

That Voltaire was not only the representative but the child of his epoch, Strauss pleads as a bar against personal criticism and individual condemnation. According to him, Voltaire's character is the natural result of the spirit of the time, as well as the only fitting instrument by which the faults of that time could be made known and chastised. The corrupt time itself produced the lash with which it was scourged. Had there been only a pure, calm, dispassionate temper in Voltaire's attack, it would have availed nothing; for it would have been like a flame within the wire network of the safety-lamp, and no explosion would have taken place in the poisonous and deadly gasses. Only his sharp, bitter, cutting sarcasm and contempt could pierce old abuses to the heart, and open the way for higher truths.

In this respect, Voltaire was, indeed, the man for the hour. He seemed denuded of all reverence and all reserve; and contempt seemed his native air. His faults of temper, his lack of conscience, his bristling self-love and overweening conceit, served him well. We will endeavor to be as grateful as we can for the hail and the pitch, the brimstone and the fire; but they *are* hail and pitch and brim-

stone and fire still. We will do our best to acknowledge that debt of gratitude we owe to him;
for, according to Lord Brougham, "no one can be
named since the days of Luther to whom the spirit
of free inquiry — nay, the emancipation of the
human mind from spiritual tyranny — owes a more
lasting debt of gratitude."

It is hard, however, for us to separate the work
done from the personal merit or demerit of the
instrument through which it was done; but that
separation must be made if any just verdict is to
be rendered in regard to the work itself. Motives, character, individual excellence or worth-
lessness, have no bearing upon this except as
furthering or detracting from the results brought
about. With the confident audacity of an unmeasured reliance upon his splendid talents, his
shrewd cunning, his perception of the vice, the in-
humanity, the weak points, of the assumptions of
the Roman Catholic Church, — everywhere hostile
to freedom of thought, to true nationality, to the
unity of the family and the State, to all advance in
science, all social changes not in the line of its
own ecclesiastic dogmas and claims to domina-
tion,— Voltaire led the attack against superstition;
the infamous foe, as he regarded it, of the human race. He was fettered by no scruples of con-
scientious care lest he should wound this tender
sentiment or that holy trust; for he was without
any conception of the meaning of those deep religious tendencies which pardon everything to that

which is associated with their rise and their vivacity of impressiveness. He was carried by no flight of genius into those higher visions which belong to creative power; so that all he wrote found ready ears and recipient response. So obtuse was he to the noblest unfoldings of the genius of religion and poetry in the past, that the Gothic cathedral was to him but "a fantastic compound of rudeness and filigree." This highest quality of genius would have been a fatal obstacle to such a work as Voltaire was the instrument in effecting, and would have incapacitated him from being the successful leader in that forlorn hope of attacking the stronghold of ecclesiastical absolutism which banished, imprisoned, cursed, and tortured wherever there was opposition to its claims. That opposition was everywhere; for it was the rising spirit of modern society seeking to establish itself on the basis of humanity and common-sense.

That Voltaire held only a secondary place among the world's great leaders and representative men was the chief factor in his success. Comte was right in calling him "the most distinguished type in history of the *provisional* laborers in intellectual and social reform,— one who to the remotest posterity will hold a position entirely unique, in whom there was the most admirable combination, such as may never again be found, of those various secondary qualities of mind which so often wear the seductive guise of original genius."

Here is the key to that wonderful mastership,

that phenomenal greatness, of him who has been called "Voltaire, the king." His work against the mighty foe of human freedom, of independent nationalities, of the sanctuary of conscience and spiritual personality, has not yet come to an end; but it is in far different hands, and must be accomplished by far different methods. The mocking laughter dies away; the fire and the whirlwind have cleared the atmosphere so that we can now listen to the still, small voice that speaks within the inmost soul, and cheers every sincere longing "for God, freedom, and immortality."

# IV.

## NEMESIS IN GREEK TRAGEDY.

"CROSSING a bare common in snow-puddles at twilight, under a clouded sky, without having in my thoughts any occurrence of special good fortune, I have enjoyed a perfect exhilaration. Almost *I fear* to think how glad I am." Thus, from his own relation to primitive nature, spoke Emerson, our modern seer. The gladness was too great for the small mortal cup, and it seemed almost an invitation to the tempest that should follow.

The old Greek felt the same trembling of the balance between joy and fear, and Nemesis was born. With the generality of men the gladness comes, not when wading through snow-puddles, but in flowery meadows and grassy paths; not at twilight and under a cloudy sky, but in the broad sunshine and glow of day. The Greek saw that nothing was stable, nothing permanent in the heavens above or in the earth beneath; and out of his subjective experience he created an objective character, exalting the human appearance into a divine personification. It was not for man with his limitations of state, nature, life, and means of good, to be too prosperous, too knowing, too happy, too powerful.    Says Herodotus: "The divinity, having given a taste of the sweetness of life, is found afterward to be envious of that happiness." If man were completely healed of disease, of course Pluto would be robbed of his rightful prey; and therefore Esculapius, the healer of the sick, is stricken down by the thunderbolt of Jove.    Prometheus, who takes pity on the shivering, helpless race of man and steals for him the spark of fire from heaven, is chained and tortured.    Solon tells Crœsus that "the divinity is always jealous, and that time constrains men to see and to suffer many things that they would not willingly see and suffer."    Amasis says to his friend Polycrates, "Your *too great* good fortune does not please me, knowing as I do that the divinity is jealous.    I cannot remember that I ever heard of any man, who, having been continually successful, did not utterly perish."    Herodotus puts into the mouth of Artabanus, when discussing with Xerxes the expediency of the war with Greece, these words, in which the aspect of the deity toward man, or the divine Nemesis, is clearly stated: —

"Do you not see how the deity always hurls his thunderbolts against the loftiest buildings and the highest trees?    For the deity strikes down everything that is exalted too high; and a large army is often destroyed by a small one, when the jealous deity strikes them with panic or lightning, so that they perish unworthily, because the deity will not suffer any one but himself to cherish lofty thoughts."

So it is, that, transferring his own subjective experience, his own standard of judgment, to the government of the world, before he has recognized the operation of essential laws working in himself and in all human souls, man sees a deity envying human prosperity, jealous of his own glory, crushing out pride, abasing high thoughts, and bringing the creature of a day to a sense of his nothingness and his low estate.

There were set bounds, impassable to human strength, skill, wisdom, enjoyment; and to go beyond this bound in any respect was to brave the higher, divine power, and to offend that majestic leveller, that equal distributor,— Nemesis. The gods alone were the blessed ones, to whom no decay or death came, and it was not for man to rival the gods. Pindar prays that the victor, whose success he celebrates, may not excite against him the jealous Nemesis.

This is the language from a human point of view: it is apparent, not absolute truth. But with the growth of the Greek man comes also the growth of the Greek gods. The Hellenic ideal is harmony, proportion of parts; nothing in excess, the golden mean, moderation in all things; no excess in feeling, life, or art; the keeping of due bounds in living, in behavior, in utterance, in thought. Within these bounds Nemesis was powerless; but outside of them there was no escape from her omnipotent clutch. Aristotle, with his usual perspicacity, calls Nemesis "the act of moral judgment awarding what is due." The emotion felt in awarding this judgment will derive its quality from the nature of him who feels it. The malicious man rejoices at the misfortunes of others; the envious man grieves at the prosperity of all but himself; while, holding the mean between these extremes, the just man, inspired by Nemesis, grieves only at the prosperity of the unworthy. Thus in Greek thought the fierce, envious, malicious gods recede, and a divine power, an all-adjusting righteous element, a divine Nemesis, presides over human destinies.

> " Mountain tall and ocean deep
> Trembling balance duly keep."

As Saint Victor [1] says of Zeus, that, before he became condensed into the grand form of King of Olympus, he wandered in the storms of air,— so we may say of Nemesis, that, before she figured as the celestial maiden with the right hand pointing to the breast, the eyes cast down in reflective meditation, and the left hand holding a bridle, or a chalice carried with even hand so that no drop was spilled, — before this crystallization into the expression of a harmonious law of moral order took place, Nemesis was the implacable Erinnys, the stern Dice, the inexorable Adrasteia, raging with envy at human success, striking down every head as it emerged from the low mortal level; a child of night or of Erebus, a formless dread impending over what was great and beautiful and strong.

[1] P. DE SAINT VICTOR : Les Deux Masques, vol. i. p. 96.

With an intuition into the moral order of things, the poet Hesiod called Nemesis the daughter of Night, just as he called Deceit and Discord and crumbling Old Age daughters of Night; and in the popular speech whatever injustice, overweening presumption, or manifest excess of evil tendency brought about punishment was called a Nemesis, or divine retribution. An intense, personifying passion makes Electra, in Sophocles, appeal to Nemesis as the avenging spirit of the dead when Clytemnestra says that her husband had been rightly slain: "Oh hear," Electra exclaims, believing her brother to be dead, — "oh hear, thou Nemesis of the but lately dead!"

It was the Greek love of order and proportion, the Greek intuition of a principle of righteousness and moral harmony, which made Nemesis not so much a mythologic personality, though sculptured by the artist and appealed to as a deity, as a universally spread consciousness of an ever-present spirit of beauty, which thrust away the deformed and the vulgar; the spirit of majestic serenity and repose, which quieted all stormy scenes and all violent extremes; of an inward consciousness of right, the voice of God inning in the flesh, and man's sufficient consolation and strength. Socrates, in the "Republic," when about to express an opinion where he does not feel the absolute surety of truth, invokes Adrasteia, or Nemesis, that he may not say rashly and inconsiderately what would mislead himself and his friends, and so be worse than the homicide whom that implacable goddess punished. Not with impunity could the word transgressing the boundary line of the eternal realities, be uttered; and even involuntary error could not go unscathed.

Thus is developed in the Hellenic mind the idea of a moral law, pervading the world and immanent in life, which restored every disturbed equilibrium, bringing down everything to a truly human level, and suffering no excess in height or measure beyond the real standard of a common humanity. What the impartial conscience decreed, *that* was the verdict of Nemesis. That tendency of things by which secret crimes were brought to light, by which a violation of the unwritten laws against the helpless, the dead, the innocent was avenged, was a part of Nemesis. She was not so much a distinct deity with a definite form and attributes, as a concrete word by which the moral harmony of the world was indicated,—that tendency which makes for righteouness in every sphere of being; which will not let things be forever mismanaged, or what is unjust and unfair forever prevail.

The genius of Æschylus was essentially poetic, and he wrought out in massive sublimity, in grand symbols, the fearful results of violated righteousness. He dealt in colossal types of suffering and woe, of struggles with the divine ordinances, of efforts to resist the operating principles of eternal justice, of mortal weakness contending with the immortal and omnipotent Fates. With him poetry performed its true work of freeing and exalting humanity. Too much has been made of Fate as the overmastering idea in the drama of Æschylus. No dramatic action can ever come from purely passive tools; for unless the doer feels the re-bound of his own voluntary acts, he is but a wire-pulled puppet, and would be no more interesting than a rock heaved up by the resistless wave.

The spectators of the dramas of Æschylus and of Sophocles were present at scenes in which the beings whom the people regarded as supernatural powers, and whose guardian help they invoked, were represented. The destiny of the characters in these dramas was unrolled before the spectators, who were called upon to sympathize with their sorrows and their struggles. Thus, as Sellar says: "A highly idealized and profoundly religious character was imparted to the tragic representation of human passion and destiny on the Athenian stage."[1] There, in the condensed epitome of years and centuries before his eyes, was the poet's reconciliation of the divine and human in character, history, and life. It was to the Athenian what at some periods has been the inspired preacher to the Christian church, — when the listener found himself; discerned the higher meaning of life; saw the light from supernal spheres let in upon his soul, and found for what was best and noblest in himself inspiration and help.

No more effective presentation of the divine

[1] Roman Poets of the Republic, p. 124.

Nemesis as apprehended in the higher Hellenic consciousness could be given, than we have in the "Persians" of Æschylus. How shall the poet deal with this subject, the overthrow of the Persians, — a subject so near to and so much a part of the audience themselves, — in order to throw around its details the haze of poetic illusion, and raise it into the sphere of ideal grandeur and moral beauty? He accomplishes this end by one simple stroke: he transfers the scene of the drama to the Persian capital and the Persian palace. That perspective which remoteness of time gives to deeds of the past, is here furnished by distance of space and the imaginative glories of a far-famed court, of whose magnificence and power the recent invasion had given the too-evident proof. This mighty empire had been defeated, and the Athenian spectators had themselves been the main agents of the defeat. Athens was to be glorified, and yet without awakening that overweening pride and self-confidence so fatal to soberness of thought; without calling forth the latent demons of self-exulting praise, or leading to barbarous peals of empty exhilaration. The Athenian exploits are recounted; but throughout the entire drama there is the minor key of sorrow, of pity, of deep humility, of intense commiseration and a trembling human fear, which will not suffer the triumph over the foe to be too selfish or too pronounced. The chorus of reverend men left to keep watch and ward over the kingdom expresses its forebodings of ill. It exults in the proud array of the kingly host, which, city-destroying, marched across the sea paved with planks and bound with cord and chain. But there steals over this bright sunlight a creeping mist; it is the thought that the gods do not allow unmingled prosperity:—

> "But when the gods deceive,
> Wiles which immortals weave
> Who shall beware?
> Who, when *their* nets surround,
> Breaks with a nimble bound
> Out of their snare?"

Urged by the same presentiment of ill, the aged queen of Darius and mother of Xerxes comes to consult these ancient, trusty Persian men in regard to the dreams that have nightly disturbed her rest since her son departed with the army to "bring destruction on Attica." They advise her to supplicate the gods — and especially the dread shade of Darius, who had visited her in visions of the night — to send blessings on her son. She then asks them about Athens; and the praise of Athens is put into the mouth of the Persian chorus. Now enters a messenger announcing the total destruction of the Persian host; and the chorus responds with its mournful wail, as one by one each feature of the awful disaster is recounted. From the summoned shade of Darius comes the counsel not to invade Greece again; and it utters the solemn moral, —

> "Proud thoughts were never made for mortal man;
> A haughty spirit blossoming bears a crop
> Of woe, and reaps a harvest of despair.

7

Jove is chastiser of high-vaunting thoughts,
And heavily falls his judgment on the proud."

Another scene, and the final one, brings to a
climax this solemn unfolding of the divine Nemesis. Xerxes himself enters, — a lonely fugitive,
bemoaning his fate; his regal robes rent, his voice
raised in agonizing wail over himself and his country, for whose loss and misery he is to blame.
Instead of triumphal shouts, we hear these wailings of woe over the brave whose dead bodies are
washing up against the rocky cliffs of Greece, or
strewing its shores. The god on earth is trampled
in the dust; the god in heaven alone rules. The
chorus tears off its venerable beard, tears off its
folded robe, and with reiterated exclamations of
woeful lament, mingling its tears and wails with
those of the humiliated, weeping king, leaves in
solemn file the desolate stage.

How simple the means, how effective the results
of this ancient lyric tragedy! For actors, a few aged
men as a chorus, a messenger, a widowed queen, a
ghostly shade from the tomb, a fugitive king. But
sit there with the Athenian upon his bench; see
with his eyes, and hear with his ears. Listen to
the first distant thunder of mournful presentiment,
until the tempest bursts forth, and sky and earth are
enveloped in one sheet of elemental flame. Only
thus can one even faintly appreciate the effect of
such an acted poem of the divine Nemesis, with
all the accessories of fitting music and stately
dance, shrill cries and piercing strains of souls

abandoned to utmost sorrow, heads bare and bowed down over torn bosoms, with streaming tears and tottering steps, in the royal palace of the proud monarch of all those vast realms of unimaginable magnificence: truly a divine lesson, which left no room for unseemly ebullition of personal exultation, for no overweening pride of victory. There was the divine verdict against inordinate human vanity and a too towering prosperity. There was the warning, full of solemnity and pathos, to those who should despise the great laws of equal justice and of divine moderation: —

> " Let no man, in his scorn of present fortune
> And thirst for other, mar his good estate ;
> Zeus is the avenger of o'erlofty thoughts,
> A strict investigator."

But this grand national panorama is an exceptional subject in Æschylus. More in accordance with the mythologic themes generally treated is the "Oresteia," — that tale of fearful crime and its retribution; of the fury-driven avenger fleeing from the altar, and of that merciful wisdom which at last, with its sovereign grace, acquits the offender and appeases the angry and avenging deities. It is an exhibition terrible in its simplicity of an avenging, implacable outside force which will not let the offender rest quiet in his offence. The dialogue, the chorus, the entire action, conspire to unfold the ideal germs of even-handed justice contained in the shadowy and frowning myths of historic tradition. The furies of the father are appeased only to awaken the more savage furies of the mother against the son who had shed her blood. In vain does Orestes appeal to the All-seeing Sun to witness that he has justly stained his hand in a mother's blood. He is not at peace; he sees in the background the Furies with awful faces, black garments, and terrible mien, with hair of writhing snakes and scorpion whips, howling for their prey. To the chorus it is but a vain phantom, but to him they are "substantial horrors, the infernal hounds" sent from his mother. They swarm around him, they hunt him forth, and not even at Loxias' altar can he be at rest. Only the serene Goddess of Wisdom can give the casting vote which releases him from the maddening avengers.

Here we have, in a series of connected tableaux, the delineation of that process by which a righteous Nemesis secures its ends.

With Sophocles there are the same main incidents of the story; but when Orestes avenges his father's death he does a righteous act, which Apollo has commanded and approves of, and the work of Nemesis is completed. Brother and sister have acted under the inspiration and guidance of Apollo, the God of Light, the purifier, cleanser, and destroyer of noxious things. The rays of the morning sun shine upon the righteous attempt, and the chorus exults at the close that the descendants of Atreus have, by its successful accomplishment, wrought out their freedom.

The presence of a divine force of Justice accomplishing its ends is everywhere confessed, though no visible Furies scourge the offender; and in one place there is the rare but curious mention of Nemesis by name. The vile Ægisthus, seeing the covered dead body of the queen, exults over it, thinking that it is Orestes who has perished; and he dares to say that it was through the displeasure of the gods. But even his hardened and perverse soul is struck by the enormity of such an assertion, and he hastens to add, "But if Nemesis is listening, I recall my words." As if words, winged with the thought, could ever be recalled! No! Nemesis is by; Nemesis is listening; Nemesis is swifter than the word. The next moment he exultingly strips off the covering, and knows his doom.

Throughout all the dramas of Æschylus there is the same central principle. In the "Seven against Thebes," from the first stormy appeal to arms, and the rebuke by Eteocles of the maiden chorus, which humbly craves the help of protecting and loving Powers; his throwing to the winds all counsels of prudence and moderation; his headlong rashness, which cries out,—

> " Since God so hotly urges on the thing,
>     Let all of Laios' race, whom Phoebus hates,
>     Drive with the wind upon Cokytos' wave ; "

his defiance of "the fierce and hot curse of Œdipus," and of the gods who scorned his house of old, and of the warning not to hurry to shed a brother's blood, — he rushes onward to slay and be slain, to make good the blind father's curse, and lie beneath —

" A boundless wealth of earth."

In the "Suppliants" the appeal is to revere the friend of the suppliant, the guardian of the suffering, stranger guest; to honor the daughter of Zeus, — Dice, or apportioning Justice, whose wrath cannot be appeased. The prayer to Zeus, the possessor of blessedness, is to be free from ὕβρις, or wanton arrogance, that pride which he sorely hates. Upon this excess, destruction always waits.

Of the "Prometheus Bound," the only untreated extant drama by Æschylus, it is impossible to say what was the way in which the divine Nemesis was unfolded. It is but a fragment, one of three acts; and in this act Prometheus tells his own story, and gives his own version of what he did and why he suffered. He justifies himself, and hurls defiance against his seemingly unjustifiable oppressor. But the sympathizing chorus, which yet elects to share his fate, hints at that audacious recklessness which can never go unpunished, and sings of that "harmony of Zeus" which can never be disturbed by the vain counsel of mortal men. Therefore it is impossible to believe that Æschylus meant to represent, as Shelley says, Prometheus to be "the type of the highest perfection of moral and intellectual nature, impelled by the purest and the truest motives to the best and noblest ends."

All that we know of Æschylus forbids the supposition that he left, as the resultant impression of the entire Trilogy, the feeling upon the minds of the spectators that Zeus was "the successful and perfidious adversary" of man and of man's champion. Had they so understood the poet, they would have stoned him on the spot. Such a view would have been fatal to that ethical truth embodied in the idea of Nemesis. The oppressive tyrant would then have gone unscathed; the Head of the Universe would have triumphed over its righteous laws. No, it could have been no "feeble" reconciliation which the poet brought about; in it the sovereign righteousness must have triumphed in a way to satisfy the higher demands of a purely moral consciousness. Even the self-will of the mightiest Titan must be brought into harmony with the order of the universe.

When Æschylus began his career as a dramatic poet the superhuman, gigantic figures of the mythologic age had not attained a human and every-day form. He seizes upon a few simple, grand outlines, and with bold, unerring stroke depicts them to the eye, without stopping to assign motives, to reconcile inconsistencies, to multiply or explain details. He deals with colossal figures, vast masses of light and shade, and throws the light of divine truths upon man from the outside with a lens of demonic and prophetic power.

But Sophocles — and Æschylus himself before his death — began to use a finer art; to discriminate more nicely as to motive, impulse, purpose, and character. This was in the natural course of dramatic evolution, as the epic and the lyric elements became fused together into a higher synthetic form. It was also in accordance with the political and social development of Athens, where everything was full of life, everything changing and interworking to new issues and fresh solutions of the eternal problems of morals and religion.

In Sophocles the harmonious, serene, all-reconciling character of his poetry was the natural expression of the harmonious and serene character of the man. In his view no excess, no morbid contest of passions, no eccentric outburst of moods, confused the rhythm of that eternal law which was not outside but inside the soul of man. Antigone can calmly violate the highest human authority, but cannot sin against the supreme mandate of her own soul. She can resign every earthly joy, she can die: "to please the living is for a moment, to please the dead is forever." Sophocles never parades the internal contests of the soul in order to attain some sensational end; he unfolds them only so far as is necessary for the attainment of purification and repose. With him health must come from elevation into a purer air; peace, from the resolution of elemental discords into a central harmony. The law in man punishes pride, restrains arrogance, discloses guilt, — that eternal law "which no mortal established, and which no old age can impair." The Furies themselves are lulled to sleep by his song. Like Æschylus, he was penetrated through and through with the sacred character of his work; so that Landor is right when he makes him say of himself: "I am only the interpreter of the heroes and divinities who are looking down upon me."

Nothing can be more misleading than the attempt to make characterization a prominent feature of the Greek drama, as it is undoubtedly of Shakspeare's plays. In Æschylus and Sophocles there is no depicting of various and manifold traits with delicate and subtile shadings of motive, impulse, and tendency. The individualities are strong and pure; but they are not real flesh and blood, changing with the changing breeze and tinged with varying hues, as the fresh life-current, welling up from the heart, retards or quickens the pulse and sends a passing cloud or sunlight over the countenance. They are not forms subject to every skyey influence, whose real feelings, moods, and purposes are subjects to speculate about, like those of any actual, living person whose character assumes a different aspect according to the different point of view. The personages are plastic forms, expressing a few definite, well-defined qualities simply and directly, in accordance with the simplicity and directness of the time. Schiller said: "It seems to me that the characters of Greek tragedy are more or less ideal masks, and not individual persons." But their real nature is more clearly designated by Hegel, who says:

"The personages are neither what we in the modern sense term characters, nor are they pure abstractions; but they stand between these two extremes,— firm figures, which *are* just what they are, and nothing else, without any internal collision, and without any mingling of conflicting elements; absolutely determined characters based upon some definite and simple moral state." That is, there is individual character, but all forces are excluded except those which work in a straight line; and therefore no higher calculus is needed to determine the direction and movement of the impinging objects. There are no infinite gradations of guilt and mental suffering, of waverings and conflicts of purpose, of infirmities of resolve, of gradual hardening of conscience and obscuration of the inner light. Our interest is not that of an overpowering personal sympathy, our judgment not distracted by various and complex views of life and conduct. In the modern drama there is the free play of individual states, feelings, idiosyncrasies of mood and temperament, personal traits and complex situations, with new combinations springing from the action and reaction of colliding views of life and duty. The ancient heroes and heroines go straight to the goal, and are but little affected by the currents and counter-currents proceeding from varying humors and interjected side-interests of a large number of dramatic personages.

Now, it is because of this varied and complex nature of Shakspeare's dramas, because he works

out his results from so many different foci, because he never expresses in didactic form the
great moral lessons at the heart of his mimic representation,—it is because of these things that the
reality of a conception of retributive justice as a
central idea is denied to his tragedy. Even J. A.
Symonds makes this assertion. But he accounts
for it by assigning as a reason the "*continued* treatment of one class of subjects,—namely, the mythological, which remarkably exhibited the working of
a retributive justice." Yet how can this be, when,
with this "continued treatment" the idea almost
disappears from Greek tragedy, and is to be found
most vividly presented in Æschylus himself, the
earliest of the tragic poets? In Euripides, the last
of the mighty three, the idea has almost faded out,
and passionate caprice, intense subjective tendencies, dominate the entire treatment of the material.
In his presentation of the well-worn, threadbare
subjects there is the romantic abandonment to
impulse and wayward feeling, keen psychological
analysis, eloquent dissertation, and beautiful simple
narration; but there is no sureness of eternal vision
and no instinctive fidelity to those spiritual laws
which made the very warp and woof of the being of
Æschylus, as they did of the ancestral myths. No!
it was the genius of Æschylus that sculptured out
of this marble quarry those forms of transcendent
justice, and gave to the popular consciousness
those awful gods who, "not of to-day or yester-
day," have ruled the world.

## V.

## THE POPE IN "THE RING AND
## THE BOOK."

THE old Pope, trembling on the verge of the grave, has waded through all the dreary documents on that dreary winter's day. Some of them are dreary enough, even after they have been shaped into what the poet fancies is a ring; but what must they have been in the rough? Innocent XII. has read them all through; and what next? He will look to the history of his predecessors, so that he may take instruction from them, and haply get some precedent in the case. The Persian king, Artaxerxes or Ahasuerus, made search in the book of records of his fathers, and finding evidence enough of the rebellious spirit of Jerusalem, decreed that a stop should be put to the rebuilding of its walls. So the Pope would find in the history of his predecessors some light to guide him in the decision he was to make as the last court of appeal, whether Guido Franceschini and his accomplices should be snatched from death.

In searching thus to see what God had gained or lost by having a vicar or representative in the world, the good Pope comes across a curious precedent, not very well adapted to make him confi-

dent in his own judgment, or secure in his own
infallibility as Pope, and voice of the unchange-
ble One. He finds a ghastly decree against Pope
Formosus after he was dead and buried; then dug
up and seated in Saint Peter's chair; then condemned, and the corpse cast into the Tiber; then
next year the sentence reversed, and the Pope re-
poped, and his condemner pronounced accursed;
then this judgment condemned, and Formosus
again cast out; then, lastly, the final sentence
given, Formosus decreed a holy man, and all his
dignities restored. Which of all these was the infallible decree? In which did God speak? Truly,
a puzzling conundrum to the anxious seeker after
historical precedent.

But the Pope gets what is better than any literal
example or direct precept: he gets inspiration,
courage, light. He sees that the old Formosus
condemned, absolved, condemned and absolved
again, was no wise affected in reality by all the
varied processes of embalming, dislocation, de-
vouring by fishes, miraculous restorations, and
final reinstatement as a corpse in good standing,
as a Pope of immaculate fame. Not all these con-
demnations could touch the soul of the man.
Courage, then, and stand by thy soul, now when
thine own turn has come to give judgment! Now,
he, Pope Innocent, is to speak in God's name; to
speak the word which is to push "a poor, weak,
trembling, human wretch" over the edge into "the
awful dark," or to hold out the hand and draw him

back. It is winter outside: it is yet more sombre winter in the Pope's soul, as the darkness of evening shuts from sight the dismal documents. But his course is clear; his mind is made up; he has no irresolution. Yet he pauses before he rings the hand-bell and makes known his irrevocable sentence. Why? Because he may be fallible in his judgment? Or does he fall back upon his infallibility as God's vicegerent, as sitting in Christ's seat? Never this plea from first to last. He is a man, and as a man may possibly err. But if he err, it is in ignorance; and that is "his sorrow, not his sin."

No morbidness of conscience is in the sound-hearted old man, though he is an ecclesiastic; he makes strenuous use of all the faculty God has given him, and not God himself can ask more. God judges by the intent and not by the outward act; God knows the integrity of his heart, and therefore he has no fear at all. It may be the last act of his trembling eighty-six years; but in that last act will be tasted the true product of his heart and soul. The method of judgment taken, the tribunal appealed to by this soul laden with "the cark and care" of the whole world is the pivotal thing so far as the Pope is concerned. It is, in fact, a practical commentary on these words of Emerson: —

"Whoever looks with heed into his thoughts will find there is somebody within him that knows more than he does, — a simple wisdom behind all acquired wisdom ; something not educated or educable, not altered or alterable ; a mother-wit, which does not learn by experience or by books, but knew it all already ; makes no progress, but was wise in youth as in age. More or less clouded, it yet resides the same in all, — saying ay, ay ! or no, no ! to every proposition. Its justice is perfect ; its look is catholic and universal, its light ubiquitous like the sun."

Now, who is this somebody within him that knows more than the aged Pope with all his apostolic functions, more than the vicar of Christ with all his outpoured spiritual illumination? It is to his "ancient self," plain Antonio Pignatelli, as was his name before he was Pope, that he will state the reasons why he finds Guido reprobate, and not to be saved from the clutches of the law:

> " Wherefore, Antonio Pignatelli, thou,
> Mine ancient self, who wast no Pope so long,
> But studied God and man the many years
> I' the school, i' the cloister, in the diocese
> Domestic, legate-rule in foreign lands, —
> Thou other force in those old busy days
> Than this gray ultimate decrepitude, —
> .     .     .     .     .     .     .     .     .     .
> Thou, not Pope, but the mere old man o' the world,
> Supposed inquisitive and dispassionate, —
> Wilt thou, the one whose speech I somewhat trust,
> Question the after-me, this self now Pope,
> Hear his procedure, criticise his work ? "

Here, verily, is the appeal from Philip drunk to Philip sober; from representative Pope to the manly self before Pope was thought of! With

this electric light steadily burning, far-flashing
its beams into every dark corner, every foggy
nook, every cobwebbed hole, he brings out trick-
ster and vermin, wolf and fox, forger and coward,
fool and murderer, — all in one. So also is revealed that choice flower of earth, that blossom
"gathered for the breast of God" : —

> " See how this mere chance-sown, cleft-nursed seed,
>     That sprang up by the wayside, 'neath the foot
>     Of the enemy, — this breaks all into blaze,
>     Spreads itself, one wide glory of desire
>     To incorporate the whole great sun it loves,
>     From the inch-height whence it looks and longs."

Then what a humanly smile sweeps across the
rigid papal mask, as the good soul calls up the
vision of the masquerading Caponsacchi, stripped
of all his conventional priestly clothing, and leap-
ing at the first call into the arena to fight for God!
What clear insight, on this basis of a purely human
touch, in separating the apparent from the real, the
surface from the substance! Yet at last comes
the doubt whether this light may not be from a
coal blown bright by his own breath, and not be at
all the light of the upper sky! Instead of a celestial star there may be only a burning coal!

A quick, cold thrill creeps over him, and his
tense nerve slackens at the doubt. Why not face
it, and look for that higher light from which his
own little spark of intelligence is drawn? However little, this mind of man is in its degree the
representative, "though but an atom-width," of

the measureless intelligence. However small this earth, it became among all the peopled stars the stage for that transcendent act of self-sacrificing love, which makes the seeming deficiency of goodness in the work of God equal to the manifest intelligence and strength. He believes in this divine story of unlimited self-sacrifice, and finds nothing lacking of "perfection fit for God." All the pain of life is meant to bring out the moral qualities of man, to make him loving and pure, and to form the moral sense which grows by exercise. Man is to make a fairer world than he finds here; and so Pompilia is not lost, and Guido may be saved in that large life which awaits those who pass out of this small world. This earth is but the starting-point, not the goal.

But this thought terrifies him, that those who profess to know the worth of the priceless pearl dredge only for whelks and mud-worms,—as the archbishop, the bare-foot monk, the Convertites, the women meant to help women, who yet for a little expected inheritance slander the sainted mother and would rob her child. Is this the outcome of "seventeen hundred years since God died for man"?

Then, further, it forces itself upon him that love and faith leap forth to-day, not under the authority of the Church, but at the call of purely human instinct. The Christians,—into what corners have they slunk? But the light will still burn. The clouds are sun-suffused, their soft

8

streaks are beautiful; and that which seems weakness is but the incentive to humanity; so that the
divine act of self-sacrifice, never ending, always
begins for man.   Then all is light.

> " So does the sun ghastlily seem to sink
> In those north parts, lean all but out of life,
> Desist a dread mere breathing-stop ; then slow
> Reassert day, begin the endless rise."

The old Christian heroism, he thinks, is impossible, perhaps, because there is such an ignoble
confidence and cowardly assurance in the truth as
being already won.

But what vision rises before him?  He sees the
dawning of that terrible eighteenth century, whose
mission it is to shake all the pillars of assured
faith, to shake that belief in *the report* which has
been substituted for belief in *the thing* that was
reported, and to correct the old portrait, "the
man's God by the God's God in the mind of
man."   Ah, what a morris-dance for the selfishness, the greed, the passions of men !

But he will smite with all his strength, in spite
of the pleas to a sense of honor and an educated
taste; to privilege of the clergy and interests of
the Church; to claims of culture and civilization;
to the necessity of the husband's supremacy over
the wife; to the appeal for him to spare his own
closing life this bloody setting, and to spare the
Church from incoming Luthers, Calvins, and Mo-
linos; to win the benedictions of the city.   In
spite of all, he gives the order for the execution

of the criminals in the most public place, — the
People's Square.   The very suddenness of the fate
may save the murderer's soul; for, he says,—

> " I stood at Naples once, a night so dark
> I could have scarce conjectured there was earth
> Anywhere, sky or sea, or world at all :
> But the night's black was burst through by a blaze ;
> Thunder struck blow on blow, earth groaned and bore
> Through her whole length of mountain visible.
> There lay the city thick and plain with spires,
> And, like a ghost disshrouded, white the sea.
> So may the truth be flashed out by one blow,
> And Guido see, one instant, and be saved."

Wonderful Pope! whose natural force and whose
true instinct the Augustinian monk, in his sermon,
may well call a miracle.   It would be indeed a
miracle to have such a Pope; for it would put the
good Innocent of the seventeenth century in the
poetic chair of the stalwart leader of the spiritual
thought of the nineteenth century.   No Pope that
ever yet gave the papal benediction would thus
have threaded the maze of theological vatication.
No twelfth Innocent has here contributed his quota
to that golden ring, though to say so is to deny
the claim of dramatic transposition.   But it is the
genuine Robert Browning who has sat on the papal
throne, and laid down a precedent which, I am
afraid, the infallible successor of Saint Peter will
be very sure not to follow.

# VI.

## BROWNING'S "IN A BALCONY."

"Now!" "Not now!" So ring in staccato tones
the plea and its denial. The man aspires "to live
in harmony with truth;" the woman fears that the
open truth will be their ruin. Why cannot the
present life of stolen interviews, of secret confi-
dences, which neither queen nor court suspects, be
continued? The woman — politic, afraid of meeting the direct consequences of open avowal — becomes the adroit casuist, the convincing pleader
for indirection, and for averting the manly avowal
of their mutual love. The forecasting prudence
offers a compromise, and that compromise is
reluctantly assented to by the lover.

Evidently we have here an utterance different
from that which came from another moon-lit balcony, where the loving heart expresses itself in the
words, —

> "And all my fortunes at thy feet I 'll lay,
> And follow thee, my lord, throughout the world."

Yet here, too, in this dramatic sketch by the
great poet, we *do* have a love-tragedy, — tragedy
in every sense. A tragedy is something more than

a fatal result, a death, an inevitable stroke from the outside. Death comes to all, but we do not therefore call it a tragedy, whether accidental or necessary. Disappointment, thwarting of highest purpose, wreck upon some lee-shore, may be tragic enough; but the simple happening of these events, though accompanied by untold sufferings and anguish, does not of itself constitute a tragedy in the true sense of the word. In a tragedy the real element of pathos and terror is from within and not from without: it is the collision which comes from moral opposites, from irreconcilable ideals, from conflicting forces inside the soul, from the destroying tempest rushing by inevitable laws out of that quarter which had been looked to as the very source of peaceful serenity. As the end of all their joyous ecstasy of love, their hopeful schemes, their plausible plans for outwitting the conventional pressure all around them, Romeo and Juliet find the world in which they are to dwell as small as the boundaries of "one little grave." The headlong rush of a love irrespective of time and sense and earthly limitations, bore within itself the very causes that bring about the fatal end.

In the fragment before us, the collision comes from the opposite poles of that electric current which streams through all the parallel and crossing wires of the human soul and human life.

> "'T is dangerous when the baser nature comes
> Between the pass and fell incensèd points
> Of mighty opposites."

Love would have its own, but would have it in a circuitous way, — stretching a new wire, crossing and interlacing the network of wires that already existed in the actual life. The man saw clearly enough the right thing to be done, when he says, —

> "Truth is the strong thing.   Let man's life be true !
> And love 's the truth of mine : time prove the rest."

In the light and warmth of this love he would live and work, no longer hiding in corners and stealing caresses in the dark, but living a manly, open, blessed life, in which all should see, and all give due acknowledgment of, the source from which that life was supplied : —

> "I choose to have *you* stamped all over me, —
> Your name upon my forehead and my breast, —
> You, from the sword's blade to the ribbon's edge,
> That men may see, all over, you in me ;
> That pale loves may die out of their pretence
> In face of mine ; shames thrown on love fall off.
> Permit this, Constance !"

Does she permit it?   No; she even misinterprets his noble longing; she thinks he is fretting because she is not yet wholly his own; he is "stumbling at a straw," when he will risk all to gain the world's cognizance, —

> "How he loves her, and how she worships him."

Thus she would have Norbert play a false part,— "not very false, as courtiers go," but still false,— and tell the queen, whose tenderness seemed all

starved out, that he had done the great services
he had rendered out of devotion to her; and to ask
for the hand of her cousin as being the nearest
thing to her, — a ribbon valued because *she* had
worn and breathed upon it; and Norbert re-
presses his own convictions of what is highest
and best, adopts the policy of flattery and white
lies, and so uncoils the wire which will convey
safely the intensified electric current if the wire
remain unbroken and come in contact with no
other conductor.

That tragic *if!* The wire does fall upon some
other crossing wires, and they who have grasped
it in their hands writhe disfigured and lifeless
under its touch. This queen, whose tenderness
Constance thought was all starved out; this cold,
marble-encased soul; this proud thing of state and
ceremony, who will be content with the mere name
and echo of love, — is not so cold and shadowy after
all. And nowhere is the Sophoclean tragic irony
better exhibited than in the case of Constance in
the Second Part. She stands there waiting for
her lover to return, — her lover, who had adopted
her way, who had given up his own chosen plan,
and become in everything subject to her as he had
been to the queen; and instead of him the queen
herself, — the supposed stately, icy, buckram shadow
of a withered and deformed existence, — bursts in
with every nerve trembling, every organ and muscle alive, her eyes flashing, her tongue quivering
with the confession of her own love, the fulness

of her own rejoicing in the unhoped-for issue!
The almost paralyzed maiden hears the queen's
exulting proclamation that she will brush away
all obstacles, retrieve her calamitous youth, and
become the wife of the young hero of her dearest
dreams.   The poor girl drains the cup to its dregs.
She had counselled that Norbert should speak of
her as but the reflex of the queen, and is taken at
her word.   "I'll come to you for counsel," says
the queen.

> " This *he* says,
> This he does; what should this amount to, pray?
> Beseech you, change it into current coin.
> Is that worth kisses?   Shall I please him there?"

Furthermore, ·Constance is to be permitted to
choose some one whom she may love and marry.
It is, indeed, an unlooked-for catastrophe, a sudden
overcasting of the smiling sky.

Perhaps a yet more effective instance of dramatic irony is that presented in the Third Part,
when the queen, in the very noon and flood-tide
of her ecstatic joyfulness, is overwhelmed by the
calamity that no courage can overcome and no
consolation can cheer.   She had gone out, feeling
that she lived in a changed world which God's
smile had blessed, where everything was made for
happiness, and the love-lit future was all before
her in which to redeem the past.   She had had
dreams of bliss; but this was as different —

> " As these stone statues from the flesh and blood."

Her last word as she looked at "the blessed moon"
of Romeo, "the inconstant moon" of Juliet, was,

"The comfort *thou* hast caused mankind, God's moon!"

Now, however, she returns to find the lovers in
each other's arms.

But the resolute, self-composed Constance is not
wholly thrown off her balance; what the queen has
seen is all nothing but the performance of a part
as her reflex, her helper to love, and on Norbert's
part a fitting exercise of his gratitude to the queen.
She is thus self-possessed and strong, because the
highest motive has now gained full possession of
her soul. If human acting can accomplish it, all
these cross purposes shall work to bring about the
queen's desired ends. Constance will sacrifice
herself; and she explains the sudden starting away
of Norbert as a rude repulse, as if he said, "There,
now, I've had enough of you!" The kiss was but
the thanks given to the tool he had employed, and
now threw away, — "a first, as well as what was
to be the last, kiss." Turning to the queen, she
bids her take him with her own full consent. Norbert, looking upon it as a poorly played jest, asks
the queen to give him his reward, — meaning the
hand of Constance. The poor queen, still in the
meshes of her delusive dream, confesses all her
love, and offers herself to Norbert. He cannot
understand what seems only a horrible jest, and
throws himself at the feet of Constance, saying, —

> "Now you know
> That body and soul have each one life, but one:
> And here 's my love, here, living at your feet."

The queen is silent, but we see her there grasp-
ing fiercely the balcony, "glaring with panther's
eyes" at Constance, who in her turn succumbs
and glares back again.   Now Norbert understands,
and says: —

> "Was it your love's mad trial to o'ertop
> Mine by this vain self-sacrifice?   Well, still
> Though I should curse, I love you.   I am love,
> And cannot change!   Love's self is at your feet!"

The queen retires, as well she may.   The lovers
now find each other out, and in the joyfulness of
perfect trust await the coming of the guard to
stamp upon their love the black seal of death.

At last the swan-song of love, here as it is not
always, is, —

> "And all my fortunes at thy feet I 'll lay,
> And follow thee, my lord, throughout eternity. "

Or, as Constance expresses it, we are here "on
the breast of God."

But the Philistine asks for the moral of it all.
Well, he may surely see that to bring about external success it is not best always to go cunningly
to work, inasmuch as truth is the sure thing, the
strong thing, in this universe of God.   Constance
was false to love; for she could imagine, one moment at least, her lover to be so base as to give his

hand for a crown, and barter her away for any living thing.  Norbert was false to his own clearly-
seen, noblest ideal of manliness and truth; and
between "the fell, incensèd points of mighty opposites" both must be consumed.  Constance has
brought about the very ruin which she feared her
lover would effect by his straightforward "now."

But is this the final result?  Is this all that
comes of their struggle in the flesh, their human
contact, and their mutual aspiration?

No, this is not all by any means.  The ruin is
but the tearing down of the scaffolding, to show the
perfect proportions of the building within.  What
matter now, as the unsightly structure falls, how
much labor was spent in gathering together its
beams and planks, in nailing fast its floors and
stagings?  Down it all goes; for the building itself
is completed, and must greet the eyes of all.  The
image used by our poet is that of the labyrinth:
why take account of the meanders, if the centre
has been reached?  "The deep plots" have all
failed to accomplish a certain external result; but
the want of wisdom which Constance thought was
the perfection of far-sightedness, and the "rashness" of Norbert, which she would guard against
as ruin to their loves, have "served them well."
The "not now" of the one and the "now" of the
other have become resolved into a higher unity
than either had dreamed of.  They are "past
harm" now, for they have attained that which perhaps could not have been attained in any other

way.   She is now his; and *that* she never was
before.   His love will never now decline into the
commonplace and vulgar life of "their five hundred friends;" for now they are melted together
in the divine heat of a furnace more than seven
times heated, and without and within and around
"it is one blaze," which no time and no human
chance can ever put out.   You may call it ruin;
but it is only the ruin of the scaffolding, without
which the temple could not have been built.   You
may call it shipwreck; but the bark sinks only
"to float on another sea."

If we take Constance herself as the central figure, and name the entire action from her position
in its course of development, we should say, —

Part I.  The false move in advance.

Part II.  The surprise and almost total rout of
the advancing forces.

Part III.  The calling up of the reserves, and
victory along the whole line.

What the poet intended in the sketch we know
not, and, alas! can never know.   He has passed
beyond our mortal sight, and no one can vex his
ghost to ask what he meant, what vision of human
faculty and human destiny he saw in the creations
of his poetic power.   To him, no doubt, there was
a determined reality, though to us there may seem
something strained beyond the limits of every-day
life and common experience.   To him it was the
portrayal of a soul-crisis, an acting out of supposed
destinies, — which, granting his analysis, and look-

ing through his telescopic lens, appear to be the
onward tramp of forces that no human power can
resist. As the unfolding of such a special situation, not as a transcript of our every-day human
life, there is wonderful strength in almost every
line.

More real dramatic reproductiveness of emotion
and passion are here unfolded than in any of the
complete dramas. The dialogue is more interwoven as cause and effect, as an immediate response to the thought, and as a revelation not
merely of what is thought at the moment, but of
what has been occupying the mind. The thought
is not stated as a categorical answer to questions
that are put and to speeches that are made; but
it takes on a more dramatic life than is found in
most of the literary dramas, full as they are of
thoughtful study to readers by themselves. He
called himself " Robert Browning, writer of plays; "
but if that were all, he would not attain his right
place and his full power in the present and the
coming generations. Rather do we say, " Robert
Browning, who expressed *himself* in every line
that he wrote, whether lyric poem or dramatic
utterance; who saw under some poetic form the
mysteries that encompass our souls, and make us
bow down in reverence and in awe."

# VII.

## THE GREEK COMEDY OF MANNERS.

GREEK Comedy, as represented by Aristophanes, was the unique production of democratic Athens. It was an unbridled caricature of public and even private life,— an acted representation, in fact, of the burlesque and satirical plates of "Punch" or "Puck," when "Punch" and "Puck" are most pointed and happy in their take-off of political and social questions. Under the patronage of the State, it was a part of the Bacchus cult, like the lyric tragedy of Æschylus and Sophocles. Woman, of course, had no place in this broad and free jesting at whatever ran counter to the political, social, and personal view of the poet. Women, however, do appear in one play, in which, disguised as men, they get possession of the assembly, decree all sorts of laws, and behave in a way that would give comfort and satisfaction to the most pronounced opponent of woman-suffrage at the present day. As democracy declined, laws were passed restricting in various ways the comic poet; and about the time of Alexander the Great appeared what has sometimes been called genteel comedy, or the comedy of manners and character.

The Latin plays of Plautus and Terence are only translations or adaptations of these earlier Greek dramas. Debarred from its previous position as public critic, political teacher, and exponent of the national life, comedy lost its chorus, and was restricted to individual manners, character, and incidents.

This Comedy of Manners is best known to us through Menander, although not a play of his remains, and we become acquainted with him only through critics, scholiasts, and fragmentary scenes and quotations. He was first, as Lessing says,[1] not in point of time, but of excellence; and the transition from the old comedy to the new was gradual and almost imperceptible. This new comedy is marked by the introduction of love as a leading *motif* in the action and development of the plot. But there is a very limited range of characters and situations. The returned mercenary, with his boastful words, lavish folly, and greedy appetites; the cunning slave and unprincipled courtesan; the female slave, with whom the young man falls in love, who proves to be some well-born damsel; the unnecessary, indignant, or stupid parent, who is to be cajoled, out-generaled, and finally reduced to a willing or passive consent; the strange turns and quirks of fortune and chance; the foolish spend-thrift, the contemptible parasite, the wretched miser, the indispensable cook and purveyor-general to appetite,—these intrigued, crossed and re-

[1] LESSING: Dramaturgie, vol. ii. p. 173, *note.*

crossed one another's path, and formed the general stock in trade of comic writers.

In this later comedy chance plays the same part as fate in tragedy; human follies are contemplated from the ridiculous side, and nothing comes to a serious and earnest issue. This comedy deals with surface-appearances, not the solemn realities of life. It is not a higher Nemesis with its thunder-bolt, the bursting forth of forces long pent-up which find their equilibrium in the darting electric spark. It is the same element playing in auroral gleams and broad sheets of harmless flashings across the firmament. It is no crisis, or judgment-day, but a pleasant tournament, or a market fair, where the sudden shower determines no fate of contending armies, but only dampens the mirth a little and wets some of the fine uniforms and gallant plumes.

In Shakspeare we have both tragedy and comedy; not only in separate dramas, but inextricably interwoven in the same scene,— just as it is in life, where the sublime and the ridiculous, the severely grand and the grotesque, tear and smile, primal granite and tenderest flower, are found close together. Mr. Ruskin has so aptly spoken of this characteristic, that I quote his words:—

"Shakspeare has been blamed by some few critical asses ior the raillery of Mercutio, and the humor of the nurse in Romeo and Juliet; for the fool in Lear; for the porter in Macbeth; for the grave-diggers in Hamlet, etc.; because, it is said, these bits interrupt the tragic feeling. No such thing. They enhance it to an incalculable extent; they deepen its degree, though they diminish its duration. And what is the result? That the impression of the agony of the individuals brought before us is far stronger than it could otherwise have been, and our sympathies are more forcibly awakened; while had the contrast been wanting, the impression of pain would have come over into ourselves, and our selfish feelings instead of our sympathy would have been awakened, the conception of the grief of others would have been diminished, and the tragedy would have made us very uncomfortable, but never have melted us to tears or excited us to indignation. When he whose merry and satirical laugh rang in our ears the moment before faints before us with 'a plague o' both your houses! they have made worms' meat of me!' the acuteness of our feeling is excessive; but had we not heard the laugh before, there would have been a dull weight of melancholy impression which would have been painful, not affecting."

As the Grecian drama was a purely indigenous product, it shows us most clearly the moral, social, political, and religious character of the times. It is a mirror faithfully reflecting the nature of the period, if not Nature herself. In tragedy there was the spirit of worship, ideal aspiration, the embodiment of the national cultus, and its roots were intertwined with the national life itself. As the mythology became dissolved into clouds and mists by the analysis of the philosopher, the travesties of the comedian, and the indifference of epicurean indulgence and luxurious sensuality, the grand ideal representation palled upon the taste. The serious drama ceases to be picturesque, symbolical, positive in its tone, and becomes subjective, analytical, and didactic. The style approximates to prose, and is more like the style of ordinary life. Comedy, too, passes through the same transitions. When the gods are no longer believed in, they cease to be comic material. Broad caricatures give place to nicer delineations of character. The political drama, too, loses its edge when politics are no longer the business of the people. With popular freedom, popular criticism expires; and as public interest expires, the interest centres in the intricacy of the plot and the representation of character.

Of the thousands of plays written by different Greek authors of this school, none remains entire. The best representative was Menander of whom are found fragments in the criticisms of grammarians, in collections of gnomic sayings, and in quotations by ancient heathen and Christian writers. No writer attained a greater circle of enthusiastic readers; and according to the essay ascribed to Plutarch comparing Aristophanes and Menander, no dramatist was so frequently exhibited on the stage. Plutarch contrasts the refined style of Menander with what he calls "the blustering, mean, obscure, turgid, strutting, prattling, and fooling style of Aristophanes," whose personages, he says, "do not express themselves according to character, stateli-

ness in the prince, energy in the orator, meanness
of language in a low station, sauciness or pertness
in a tradesman," etc. Menander's style is, on the
contrary, "proportioned to every sex, condition, and
age." As if Aristophanes' drama were intended
to be one of character, manners, or private life!
We might as well object to the pineapple because
it is not an orange. Yet as showing the opinion of
Menander held in the second century, when all his
plays were entire, this testimony is exceedingly
interesting. Plutarch says further: —

"Menander has shown himself sufficiently charming,
being the sole reading, topic, and discussion at theatres,
schools, and entertainments, his poetry being the most
universal ornament that was ever produced by Greece.
For what other reason should a man of learning and
talent frequent the theatre, except to hear Menander?
And when are the theatres better filled than when his
comedies are performed? And at private entertainments
among friends, to whom do the meats and the drinks
more justly give place? To philosophers also and hard
students Menander is a rest from their lecturing and
their thinking, and entertains their minds with pleasant
and cool meadows amidst the shade of trees and re-
freshing breezes."

The comedy of Menander must have been for
generations the best exponent of the moral and
social conditions of his time. In modern times
the nearest approximation to it is that of Molière
in France. It represents classes of characters

rather than distinct individualities; types, and not
separate personalities.    In ˙Aristophanes, even,
who represents the old comedy, — a broad caricature of manners, social tendencies, politics, and
contemporary men and events,— there is already
to be perceived after the parabasis and chorus are
forbidden, an attempt to delineate character.    But
there was no room for any nice delineation or delicate shading on his canvas, covered as it was with
groups of massive forms.    Everything was picturesque, imaginative, fantastic, an acted series of
broadest caricatures, wherein the only limit was
that the very extreme of the ludicrous was reached,
and one could laugh no more.    This end was attained by dissolving all into a universal jest.    With
the general spread of philosophic thought, however,
and the loss of interest in public affairs (that were
now managed for the people, and were wholly beyond their own interference), the intelligence and
social instincts of the rich and cultivated sought
occupation in seeing private life represented.    Man
himself became interesting to man.    The stage became a school of manners and of every-day interest.

From the names given to some of the comedies
of Menander, we may see how cosmopolitan an element had entered into Athenian life; how vastly the
sphere of experience had widened.    One is named
"The Ephesian," another "The Thessalian," another "The Carthaginian," another "The Corin-
thian."    The human element was extended; on the
stage once trodden solely by heroes and demigods

now appeared plays named "The Fisherman," "The Pilots," "The Husbandman," "The Shipmaster."

The grand ideals of tragedy were now out of place. What echo could the austere forms of self-sacrifice, the heroic models of patriotism and religious faith find in that ennuyed and enslaved community, whose greatest orator was Demetrius Phalereus, and whose greatest philosopher was Epicurus? Instead of the intense heat of national patriotism and traditional belief, there was a more pervasive sentiment of humanity and interest in man as an individual being. He appeared now, not as the politician, the demagogue, the general, the flatterer of the people, the public poet, and the philosopher, but in the various forms that made up the private life of the community. Youthful lovers, old misers, boastful soldiers, parasites, flatterers, women of pleasure, victims of fraud and superstition, dupers and their dupes, enemies and friends, guardians and wards, — all these found voice and fitting form in the comedy of Menander.

The thin and meretricious comedies of Terence give only a partial idea of the style and contents of the plays of Menander. In the Greek dramatist love, honorable and domestic, appears as a *motif*, and is widely sundered from the loose relations that make the staple of the Latin poet. The outlines of three comedies are given by the scholiasts, and these show that the drama had taken up the representation of domestic and home life among the people.

One of these plays is called "The Plokion," or "Wreath." Here two marriages are contrasted, — the one ill-sorted and turning out badly, in which the husband, tempted by a large dowry, had taken to wife a woman deformed both in body and mind; the other a genuine love-match, crowned at last by a happy union.

Another play, whose plot is outlined, is called "The Treasure." In this, a rich father leaves his property to his spendthrift son on condition that at the end of ten years funeral honors should be paid to himself at a tomb already erected in one of his possessions. The son spends lavishly his property, and even disposes of the field in which was the tomb, reserving to himself, however, the right to visit it and perform his duties according to the terms of the will. When the tenth anniversary comes round, the son, accompanied by the purchaser, goes to the tomb, which is now for the first time opened. Therein a casket is found containing a large treasure, from which the play takes its name. The purchaser claims it as being a deposit which he himself had made, to hide it from thieves and marauding soldiers. The matter is brought before the courts, where the cause is tried; and on opening the casket a letter of the deceased to his son is found, and decision is given accordingly. In this letter the father assigns as his reason for making such an arrangement, that the son's filial regard would be tested, and rewarded or punished according as he complied with or disregarded the condition; and if he had wasted the property he had already received, he might become wiser by the experience, and make a good use of the unexpected acquisition.

In the third play, called "The Ghost," the plot is as follows: A widower with one son marries a woman who already has a daughter, a circumstance which she does not care to make known. The daughter lives in an adjoining house, and opening from it is a door into the private boudoir or oratory of the mother, concealed by flowers and votive offerings. There mother and daughter have their meetings. The grown-up son of the husband sees the beautiful girl by chance, and takes her to be a ghost, a supernatural visitation; but he is gladly undeceived, and to the great joy of the mother leads her, as the correspondents say, to the sacred altar.

The Grecian idea of wife and mother was that of 'entire subjection and seclusion. In Plato's "Republic" woman was made the equal of man in every respect; and in the succeeding century family life became a theme for comedy, — for a revolution was going on in the very constitution of the family; the secluded and cloistral life of woman was being broken up, and her position in society was in the process of transformation.

The received Grecian idea was that the wife should be in seclusion as in a sanctuary. Laws undoubtedly at first made for her protection, and modes of living inherited from a rude and warlike

condition of society, separated woman from the
general atmosphere of thought and social inspiration.    In her seclusion she became weak, petty in
her pursuits, often rebellious under her chains,
exacting in her claims, and jealous of the authority
vouchsafed by custom and the law.    Her condition
showed, in fact, how fatal it is to perpetuate certain external forms of living after the conditions
which gave rise to them have changed.    In the
Homeric times woman was the honored equal of
man, because she was the real bond of the family
life, superintending its labors while the warrior
fought; and all her sphere was within the home.
But in the complex life of the growing city, to
limit her to the one corner of the house was to
make her a slave, — causing her to descend in
the scale of intelligence, while the husband was
ascending.    This false position of woman explains much of the moral and social degradation
of the wealthy cities of Greece.    The women who
could be companions for educated men were not
those who had been brought up in this seclusion
of the women's apartments, but were those who had
been able to acquire some instruction, and by their
freedom had shared in the civilizing and refining
elements of the time.    By the superstitious adhe-
rence to old family institutions the very life of
the family was undermined; and that position
which an advancing civilization required the wife
and mother to take, was occupied by the cultivated
and attractive courtesan.

The comedy of the time derives many of its
situations and many of its traits of character from
this anomalous condition of family life. The
woman does not take kindly to her nun-like seclusion when there is so much going on that she
would like to see and take a part in; and the man
can see only one remedy,— which is, to put more
bolts on the door, more bars on the window, and
more spies all around.

Suspicion, jealousy, cunning, and intrigue were
chronic social states. One of the married women
in Menander says: "A sensible man ought not to
imprison his wife in the back part of his house, for
then she gets to be very curious about what is going on outside. If he will only let her go about
freely, see and hear what she pleases, her curiosity is satisfied, and she is kept from evil desires. Do not men desire more eagerly what they
are forbidden to get? He who thinks to keep his
wife under lock and key is very much mistaken,
and is nothing but an idiot. When our hearts are
outside, we can get there straight as an arrow
or a bird flies; we can deceive the hundred eyes
of Argus himself. What then? Why, you are
laughed at for your pains." Thus speaks human
nature in the fourth century B. C. So it spoke in
Molière, when he says,—

"Bolts and bars cannot make wives and daughters virtuous."

Another character discusses the advantages and
disadvantages of marrying; what rights a dowry

brings with it; what a plague it is to have a rich woman for a wife, — one poor sufferer saying: "You will not marry, if you are wise. I'm a married man, and that is why I say to you, 'Don't!' You are going to sail on a sea of trouble: it is not the African Sea, nor the Ægean Sea, nor the Mediterranean Sea, where at least three vessels are saved out of thirty; but it's a sea where not a single ship floats, — not one."

Love in this comedy is of the same stamp with that which plays such an important part in the corrupt time of Charles II. and the modern sensational French drama. It is the product of a social state corrupt to the core. Yet there are some few plays where a young man sees a young girl of whom he becomes ardently enamoured. She is poor, however, or in some condition of life that forms a bar to marriage. There is the usual opposition, plots and counter-plots, hope and despair, until in the *dénoûment* the worthy young woman turns out to be of some rich or noble family, and to have been carried away in infancy, etc.; and thus all goes to the tune that has since been played so often. Some of the sentiments have a truly modern air, and, separated from their framework of circumstance, might be expressed in some comedy of manners in the England or even the America of to-day. A young man whose mother wishes to hinder him from marrying below what is considered his rank, says to her: "Always this nobility! Don't, mother, be forever setting up nobility of family! If one has no personal good quality, he falls back on his birth and the monuments of his ancestors. But what's the good of that? Every one has some ancestors, else he would not be born. If one cannot tell exactly who they are, through emigration, captivity, or some other misfortune, must he be any the less well-born than those who can say who their fathers are? The nobleman, dear mother, is he who is noble, even if he were born in Ethiopia. 'A Scythian!' they say,— 'how horrible!' Well, was not Anacharis a Scythian?"

So, too, wealth is an illusion. "I thought," says one, "that the rich slept tranquilly, and that the poor alone passed sleepless nights; but I see now that you rich folk,— you who are considered so happy,— that you are just like the rest of us. Are life and suffering, then, of the same birth?"

Another character says of wealth:—

> "Our only gods, as Epicharmus says,
>   Are air, fire, water, earth, the sun, the stars;
>   But I maintain the only useful gods
>   Are gold and silver. Set up these two
>   As household gods within your home; pray to them,
>   And all ye pray for instantly is yours, —
>   Fields, houses, hosts of servants, silver plate,
>   Friends, judges, witnesses. Give, only give;
>   The very gods are at your humble service."

Many choice sayings of Menander have been preserved by different writers, which show a spontaneous kindliness of feeling, a universal good-will, a gentle irony free from harshness, and a satire melancholy indeed, but without severity. It is this sorrowful human tenderness, this expression of sentiments belonging to the common lot of humanity, that gave Menander his hold upon his contemporaries, and has embalmed some of his sayings in the writings of succeeding generations. In translation their aroma escapes. Here are a few of them : —

"A slave, in fine, is made of as good flesh as we are."

"No noble man can be ignobly born."

"A man is a man even in slavery."

"Teach youth, for men you 'll find unteachable."

"Think all the sorrows of your friends your own."

"The conscience is the god within us all."

"Who loves himself too much is loved by none."

"To live is not to live for oneself alone."

Evidently the human had found an interpreter. The loud cry of city against city had been hushed, and that common sentiment was forming which would recognize the master-word, "He has made of one blood all nations," as the rallying cry of all noble souls. There is also the recurring strain, so frequent in Horace, of the fleeting nature of all earthly happiness, the ills of mortal life, the impartial omnipresence of the great leveller death. A shadow had passed over the clear sky and sparkling seas of Greece.

"If you would know yourself and what you are,
  Go to the tombs of the illustrious dead:
  There lie the bones of kings in common dust;
  There are the rich, the noble, and the wise;
  There beauty and renown, — one lot to all.
  Reflect, whoe'er thou art, and know thyself."

The refrain also comes, Happy he who dies when young, before old age and changing fortune have laid upon him their heavy hand.

> "For what is life, the longest life of man,
> But the same scene repeated o'er and o'er?
> A few more lingering days to be consumed
> In throngs and crowds, with sharpers, knaves, and thieves."

"Better be a dog, a horse, an ass, than be a man, and see unworthy men lord it over patient merit." Again: "You are a man, and as man you are to expect to be thrown from the highest prosperity to the lowest adversity. Bear up, then, as a man, for as yet you have suffered no extraordinary calamity."

As showing that there were some sources of consolation even in that dark hour, we hear these words, astonishing indeed as spoken on that stage as part of the acted life of that time: —

> "God is everywhere present, and sees all."

> "Without God, no man can be happy."

> "If you perform a good act, be of good hope, knowing well this, — that God is a sharer in every good undertaking."

> "God is not deaf to the just man's prayer."

It is God, and not gods, in the verse of the poet. Well may we suppose that the Apostle quoted from Menander when he said: "As one of your own poets has said, 'We are His offspring.'"

No wonder that one has said that if he could rescue any one ancient author from oblivion, it would be Menander. Quintilian says of Menander:[1]—

[1] Institutes, book x. chap. i. § 169.

"Menander admired Euripides greatly, and even imitated him, though in a different department of the drama; and Menander alone, in my judgment, would, if sufficiently read, suffice to generate all those qualities in the student of oratory for which I am an advocate, — so exactly does he represent all the phases of human life, such is his fertility of invention and easy grace of expression, and so readily does he adapt himself to all circumstances, persons, and feelings."

Again: —

"For speakers, it is necessary to assume various characters, — those of fathers, sons, soldiers, peasants, rich men and poor men, angry persons and beseeching persons, those who are mild and those who are rough. Now, in all these characters Menander observes a wonderful appropriateness, so that he has left all other dramatists of that kind scarcely a name, the splendor of his reputation throwing them entirely into the shade." [1]

There can be no more interesting study than that of the rise and progress of the Grecian drama, from its first rude beginnings in the religious chorus celebrating the exploits of the creative, nourishing, and inspiring power in Nature and life, through the various phases of its development, expressing the intellectual, social, and political changes, — a truly national drama. From it can be gained a concrete and life-like presentation of the progress and decline of Grecian faith, Grecian freedom, and Grecian manners. Throughout, we

[1] Institutes, book x. chap. i. § 71.

trace the process by which the human element is broadened and deepened, the subject-matters of thought extended and made more complex, the entire sphere of existence enlarged, and man's relations to man substituted for man's relation to the gods and other supernatural powers. It is a record of the growth of humanity; and being free from foreign admixture and influences from without, this literature is the freest exponent of the essential principles of the drama, and of its normal unfolding. An understanding of it, of the place it filled, the means by which it attained its ends, its processes of idealizing, and its resources for awakening pity, fear, sympathy, and the higher emotions of the soul, — this understanding is the best preparation for a thorough comprehension of that wonderful Shakspearian drama, in which are embodied in a form not less perfect the deeper and more universal life of our modern era.

# VIII.

## PLATO'S REPUBLIC.

THE student of Grecian history finds in it a wonderful likeness in miniature of his own times, — the same stirring interests, the same mental, moral, and social problems, that now occupy the attention of thinkers, and lovers of truth. Our age has no monopoly of social dreams and Utopian commonwealths; for Greece had them before Plato's time, in the philosophic community which Pythagoras sought to establish in Magna Græcia; and widely spread must have been the dreams and tendencies which Aristophanes satirized in his inimitable verse. No popular caricaturist would take the pains to raise a laugh against woman's participation in affairs of government and society, if such an attempt were the dream only of some one speculative philosopher, and had no general vogue. Plato's philosophic scheme stands out now as a solitary peak, but it must have been one of a mountain range. Among those small Grecian States there were indeed the seething elements of every form of government, from the unbridled tyranny of the despot to the unlicensed despotism of the wildest democracy, passing through all grades of modified aristocracies of every shade and tint of exclusiveness and worth.

The philosophers of Greece were essentially undemocratic, and excited the fears of the ignorant many, — as if philosophy were necessarily some hostile element. This led to the expulsion of Pythagoras and to the death of Socrates. The bearing of Plato towards the industrious crowd, the men of industry and toil, was one of aversion and contempt. In his view, the philosopher could be neither a man in public life nor a man of affairs; above all, he must not be engaged in business, trade, or mechanical or agricultural employments. All this was regarded by Plato as unworthy a man whose speculations must be on the highest themes, and his robes free from the dirt of earthly concerns.

Towards democratic Athens Plato felt no attraction; towards aristocratic Sparta he was strongly drawn. The Spartan institutions had existed for hundreds of years; and in their grave simplicity, their austere temperance, their indifference to pleasure and comfort, they came the nearest to the philosophic ideal. It is on those lines of Spartan exclusiveness, and the crushing out of every trace of Athenian democracy, that Plato has constructed his ideal commonwealth, — the Spartan institutions being the rough model of those in the Republic. These institutions were ascribed to Lycurgus, but they were really founded in a great antiquity, and no more belonged to Lycurgus as exclusive author than the Hebrew code to Moses. But in making artificial commonwealths this fact was forgotten; and apparently Plato thought it as easy to construct a commonwealth as to build a house. Thus have thought Utopian theorists of a later time

But in treating of Greek history, it is well to bear in mind that —

" Few distinctions are so important for a true understanding of history, as that between liberty in the classic and in the modern sense of the word. An Englishman, when he desires liberty, thinks of it as the desire of individual development, the soil on which strongly marked character flourishes most vigorously. It is doubtful whether a Greek would have understood what this means, and still more whether he would have thought it desirable. Indeed, we may say that the Greek love of liberty embodied the very opposite feeling to this. There never could have been a city less free than Sparta, according to our ideas; and evidently in making it the model of his Republic, Plato was not contemplating as a possibility the reproach that he was a foe to liberty. He and his contemporaries meant by liberty something which was compatible with any amount of despotic regulation of individual life. The ideal republic of liberty-loving Greece would have been a despotism more intolerable to modern feeling than the most despotic kingdom of modern Europe." [1]

Yet to-day these despotic features recur in many modern plans to rescue society from its evils, and produce an ideal state of well-being. The subjection of a workman to his fraternity, or Union, is

[1] The Moral Ideal. By Julia Wedgwood. P. 104.

often such as to annihilate all freedom of choice, all liberty in individual act. He voluntarily signs away his individual liberty, and is made to do what his own conscience or his own sense of expediency condemns. He gives up his own wrists and ankles to be fettered, and renounces his own freedom of action. Are we to go back to this ideal of Grecian life, in which the individual was nothing, and the city or State was all? The advance of our modern civilization began in this very separation of man from the group, of man from the citizen, and making him, whether tradesman, laborer, merchant, or soldier, a self-governing, self-respecting man. He was no longer a mere appendage to the State, not a wheel or cog in a vast machine, but a living unit, for whom all machines were made.

It is not fair to Plato to look upon his Republic, or polity of a city, as an end in itself. His purpose was not to write a treatise upon the constitution of a commonwealth, as a pattern for all who would build up States; but to furnish an illustration of that broader theme of what constitutes justice and what injustice, — the only necessary thing for an intelligent man to know. Now, as there is an analogy between the individual man and the State of which he forms a part, justice can be studied in the larger form of the State better than in the individual man. The letters composing it are there written in a large round hand, and can be more readily deciphered. The city, however, in which the form of justice can be discerned, is not any actual commonwealth, but an ideal one, constructed upon man's supposed essential nature, and governed according to the highest principles of abstract, philosophic reason. Plato sees clearly the vital connection which should exist between all the different members of a community; and he makes this general sensitiveness the test of a well-regulated State. He uses precisely the same expression that has been made use of by Shakspeare, a finger-ache being felt throughout the whole body. " In a well-regulated State," he says, " just as in the individual man, when the finger is wounded, the sensation extends throughout the whole; and by reason of the common principle of life or soul, such a State will feel that she herself is the one hurt, and will mourn with the injured member." This feeling of unity must be preserved by taking away the occasions for jealousy, rivalry, and envy. The mother will not scheme for her darling, for as there is no individual household she does not know which child is her darling. The guardian soldier will not become a tyrant, because, already supported at the public charge, he has no temptation to possess himself of the person or goods of citizens.

Plato's commonwealth is meant to be a true aristocracy, — that is, a government by the wisest and the best. These will always be the minority, " the precious remnant," of which Matthew Arnold spoke. As man is threefold in his spiritual constitution, so will the State be based on this threefold division of reason, energy (or will), and appetite (or desire). Reason is seated in the brain, energy in the breast, and appetite in the abdomen. At the basis of the State are the laborers, the cultivators of the soil, the tradesmen, — that is, all of the industrial class. Then come the soldiers, the military class; and then the governors and teachers, or official class. Through the energy of will, thought rules over and directs the lower appetites; and so the highest grade in Plato's commonwealth, the philosophers, rule over and direct the masses of the laborers and artisans through the middle class, the assistant guardians or military auxiliaries. This second grade consists of the exclusive defenders and protectors of the city, and they are absolutely free from all the cares and labors of ordinary life. The abdomen does not perform the work of the heart, nor the heart that of the brain. The highest class can engage neither in labor nor in trade: the philosopher must devote himself to thinking, the soldier to fighting, and the laborer to working. The dividing line between the castes can never be passed over, as the perfection of the whole consists in each one performing perfectly his own part. The rulers are to have wisdom; the soldiers fortitude, or courage; and the workmen temperance, or obedience.

But how is the State necessary?

The State has its foundation in human wants, and no man is sufficient for himself. From this fact, that no one is self-sufficing, springs the necessity of those who live in one place forming one community, wherein each person imparts to others what he has, and receives from others what he wants. The most pressing want is food; then lodging, clothing, etc. One man becomes a husbandman, another a builder, another a weaver, another a shoemaker, — each one having a natural fitness for some one kind of work, since each is born unlike to any other.

The "Republic" has nothing to say about the morals, the education, or the condition of the great body of the workers. They are, for the most part, slaves or aliens, — people born to eat, sleep, indulge their various appetites, and work for the support of the chosen few warriors and philosophers, who will make for them all necessary arrangements and provide for their happiness better than they can provide for themselves. The education of the guardians is to be such as will make them what Carlyle was always clamoring for, — the natural leaders and the wise helpers in the common life of the Platonic city. This care for the philosophic and military guardians was to begin before birth; for only fitting mates were to be arranged, with all care on the part of the governing body for the health and character of the offspring. No permanent life-partnerships were to be made, but the governing body was to arrange with consummate wisdom all unions of men and women under a certain age, giving to the parties a seeming choice by lot. Every element of individual love and personal affection on the part of these State guardians was to be eliminated.

They were to have no care for subsistence, and to be
free from all but the most disinterested devotion to
the welfare of the city of which they had the charge.
They were to be neither husbands nor fathers nor
human beings in any ordinary sense of those words.
They were to possess neither individual property nor
separate goods, but in a sublime sense of being a
godlike providence to the inferior race of beings
whom they protected and watched over, they were
to keep themselves secluded from the base and de-
basing world, and nourish in themselves all the arts
of wisdom, and all the means of strength. In their
childhood they were to hear none of the degrading
stories of the gods, — Plato bringing against the old
national poets the same charges that have been
brought against some parts of the Old Testament in
our day, that they degraded the deities, and gave a
wrong direction to the youthful imagination and
heart. Nothing was to be admitted in the education of these guardians which would hinder them
from becoming " pious and divine men." The
rhythm and harmony that belonged to the soul
were to be brought out by a proper training; and
thus " a man would perceive at once whatever was
bad or defective in any workmanship, would rejoice
in what was beautiful, and foster it in his soul, de-
spising what was base, even from early youth and
before reason was developed, and embracing what
partook of reason from its intimate relationship
with himself." He was to be so trained that he
would need neither lawyers nor physicians; he will

go through a course of labors, trials, and contests,
— " while yet young being subjected to various terrible tests, and then thrown back into pleasures;
tried more than gold in the fire, that he may show
whether he is in just rhythm and harmony." And
he who had been thus tried, and come out pure,
was to be appointed governor and guardian of the
State; " honors were to be paid him while he lived,
and at his death he should receive the highest
reward of public burial."

All men were brethren, it was to be taught, and
from one common mother, the earth. But those
who were able to be governors, — the real philosophers, —had gold mixed in the material of which
they were made; those who were able to be aids and
helpers had silver; and the husbandmen and artisans had iron and brass. Plato cites an oracle, which
said that whenever iron or brass should come to be
guardians the city would perish; and hence those
children who had no silver or gold in their make-up
were to be thrust down among the iron or brass to
which they really belonged. Over nothing were the
guardians to keep closer watch; and if any child
of the people should show unmistakably the vein of
gold, he was to be taken under the care of the guardians, and receive the same training as if he were
born of their number.

What arrangements were made in Plato's scheme
to develop this golden germ in any child? It does
not appear; and we may say, that if many such
children were to spring from the iron and the brass

parentage of the common herd, his whole system of exclusive education would prove a useless nullity.

Plato claims, however, that in his commonwealth every human being would find his level, and every one settle in that place for which the qualities of his nature had fitted him. Yet the same chance was not given to all, and it must be against vast odds that any shining nugget would crop out so as to be seen and transferred to the jeweller's manipulating skill.

How completely Plato derived from the institutions of Sparta the practical regulations for the education and daily life of his guardian class, to whom all government and all military powers were intrusted, may be seen from a slight consideration of Spartan customs. (1) In Sparta the citizens were obliged to eat at the common tables, living upon the simplest fare. (2) Plutarch says that Lycurgus strove to drive away from the Spartan men the vain and womanish passion of jealousy, making it quite reputable to have children in common with persons of merit; for he considered children not so much the property of their parents as of the State. (3) The Spartan father could not rear what children he pleased, but he must carry the child to a public place to be examined; and if it was weakly and deformed, it was thrown into a deep cavern called "apothetæ;" so were weak and deformed children exposed in Plato's Republic. (4) When the Spartan children were seven years old, they were enrolled in compa-

nies, and all kept under the same instruction and discipline. (5) Sparta was simply a great camp, — as
the home of Plato's guardians was but a military
barrack, without any of the adornments or con-
veniences of ordinary existence. (6) The Spartan was forbidden to engage in any business or
trade, or exercise any vocation by which wealth
could be gained; his business was to devote himself to the honor, safety, and glory of his country.
(7) The training of the Spartan girls was like that
of the boys in athletic exercises, with like contests
in wrestling and running, clothed only with a light
tunic, open at the skirts; they formed a part of
the religious and patriotic processions, and at the
public festivals sang and danced. So in Plato's Republic; the men and women of the guardian class
lived together, drilled together, — from the earliest
years being under the same superintendence, and
having the same education.

It was a doctrine with Plato, strange for that age,
that whatever man could do, woman could do also;
and that the training which was best for man was
best also for woman. There was no reason in the
nature of things, he says, why the woman should be
restricted to indoor occupations; and from the mere
difference of sex no argument could be drawn
as to fitness or unfitness for different occupations.
Only as they were properly trained could men
perform fittingly the office of guardians; and on
the same terms women also could be equally well
fitted.

But while in its positive arrangements this polity embraced many of the leading Spartan regulations, it also negatively eschewed the individual freedom of Athenian democratic ideas. For these Plato had no sympathy, and not even any tolerance. He shrank from them with all the bitterness of uncongenial temperament, and all the contempt of a philosophic superiority. That mass of people crowded in the law-courts, in the public assemblies, shouting, stamping, hooting, or applauding, — it was his aversion; and to meet their approbation was in his eyes treason to manliness and honor. "Do you not know," he asks, "that they punish with exile, fines, and death him whom they cannot influence?" The "people" was a great wild beast, which was to be kept in good humor and pleased if one would not be torn in pieces. In the degradation of a commonwealth, it passed through different forms of government until it reached democracy, on its way to an anarchy only to be superseded by some form of absolute tyranny. Whenever in a State the poor get the uppermost, banish and kill the rich, and share among themselves the magistracies and offices of State, a democracy becomes established; every one does as he pleases, and all sorts of characters spring up. Those are honored who flatter the multitude and cater to its whims.

Here Plato draws that picture which Alcibiades, or many another of the *jeunesse doré* may have sat for, — of a young man, indulging every passing desire; now getting drunk at the sound of a flute, and now drinking only water; at one time practising gymnastics, at other times lazy and idle; at one period playing the politician, at another imitating some soldier or merchant; his life regulated by no plan or law, — a truly democratic character. A democracy, in fine, is a lawless and motley affair, "giving equal rights to unequal persons."

In such a State as this, how can philosophy be cultivated, and how can the philosopher be formed? Some well-disposed youth may try to emerge from the corrupting tendencies, but being one only against the host of wild beasts, he must at last succumb and perish, without any profit to the world. Like a man sheltered from a storm of wind and dust under some wall, this man will attend to his own affairs, content to pass his life pure from injustice and corruption, and make at last a cheerful and quiet exit. And why must his life be this failure? "Because," says Plato, "he has had no suitable form of government to live under." "This is what I complain of," he says again, "that no existing constitution of a State is worthy of a philosophic nature." And so he will construct one, wherein philosophy shall have its rights, and the philosophers shall rule. Occupied with what is real and eternal, beautiful and in harmony with reason, they will imitate what they admire, and will put upon the canvas the divine pattern which they behold. And until such as these have the government of the State, he affirms, the miseries of States will not have an end.

Plato imagined he had constructed a State in which individual tastes and tendencies, personal predilections and sensual temptations, would be utterly extinguished. These guardians are not men and women, but philosophic machines moved by wires beyond their control. Their breathing can have no irregular movement, their pulse no quickening, and their cheeks no mantling blush. They are as dead to human interests as the mediæval monk, or the begging friar of the Catholic Church. They have no personal interests, but are official instruments. They have no occasion to exercise virtuous aspirations or put forth individual efforts, or be moved by pity or fear. Better the anarchy even of individual hopes and aspirations than this frozen surface of social monotony!

But however impracticable Plato's socialistic dream may appear, let it always be remembered that he was planning for no mere vulgar enjoyment, aspiring for no sensual delight, clutching no passing satisfactions of time and sense. He sought, after all, for a city which should have eternal foundations in the human soul, and whose builder should be God. His high intent shines out in the closing paragraph of his book: —

"If the company will be persuaded by me, regarding the soul as immortal and able to bear all evil and good, we shall always persevere in the road which leads upward; and above all else shall follow after justice united with wisdom, that thus we may be friends to the gods as well as to ourselves, both while we remain in this state of being, and when, afterwards, like victors assembled together we receive its rewards. And so, both here and in that journey of a thousand years, we shall be happy."

Plato, then, sought to give the model of an ideal commonwealth which should be the perfect embodiment, in the largest capital letters, (1) of Justice, or Righteousness; (2) a commonwealth in which every soul should find its own proper place; (3) in which woman should take her place on an equality with man; and (4) in which the Best, — the lovers of wisdom, the subjects of reason, the disinterested followers of truth, — should be the acknowledged rulers.

Plato's ends were lofty, and his dreams were noble; yet the edifice which he builded seems now but a sorry make-shift, because no individual plan can ever satisfy the demands of the universal spirit; because the building which *it* is erecting is of such immense proportions and such indescribable grandeur. The ideals which inspire the minds of this present hour are as grand as Plato ever mused upon; but his actual plans, suggested by the institutions and social manifestations of his day, are but a child's house of cards compared with the mighty cathedral of which the spirit of humanity is laying stone upon stone before our very eyes. Plato would have his ideal commonwealth a unit, so that the need of the remotest extremity should be at once felt and responded to by the wisest and the best; and does space make any obstacle to-day to the transmission of any sound from the remotest quarters of Africa,

Australia, and the islands of the sea? He would have all functions executed by those who were fitted for them; and for what else are we trying to-day in our demands for civil service, in our endeavors to get the best service of the best citizens? Plato would have the golden child placed among the golden men and women, though he were born of the very lowest parentage; and what are our schools for, our open careers for every son and daughter of humanity, but to supply one great bolting apparatus by which at last the great, the inventive, the skilful, the strong should find their proper place, and best minister to their fellow-men? So we might say of all the higher social tendencies at work in our community, that they are seeking to accomplish something in the direction which the purest transcendental philosopher that has ever lived set down as the only objects worthy of human pursuit. He distrusted democratic rule; but we see to-day that the true meaning of democracy is not a form of government external to the people, separate from them, like a king or an oligarchy, but it is that of a whole people governing themselves, promoting their own interests, advancing their own welfare. Not the selfishness of the few, not the passing impulses of the many, can be the permanent outgrowth of this last embodiment of the universal spirit in a political State; but that wisdom which is the inmost life of humanity is to find here its abiding home in every man's life, and every man's daily work.

# IX.

## ARISTOTLE'S "POLITICS."

ARISTOTLE'S "Politics," Prof. R. T. Ely, the economist, has recently called "one of the most remarkable books in the world's history. . . . In some respects," he says, " the most advanced political economy is a return to Aristotle." A brief survey of this great work is, then, in order in this day of " social problems."

Differing widely from Plato's poetical dream, the " Politics " may be considered the first great effort in the scientific study of society and of the elements of social well-being. Plato stood in an attitude of antagonism to the Grecian methods of life and government. He attacked the poetry, the education, and the political notions of his time. His ideal State was based upon man's supposed nature and the constitution of the soul as reason, will, and appetite. It was a true Utopia, for there was no place in all the world where it could be actually embodied; but the " Republic" presented an inspiring ideal of order, justice, and righteousness in human affairs. Aristotle's ideal is no less elevated, but his method is entirely different. Like Plato, he desires to promote the highest good of the individual in the State;

but he follows no *à priori* plan. He sets up no ideal as a necessary and universal pattern, but tries to find a reason in the nature of man and the facts of experience for Greek institutions. For the many changes that had occurred in the political forms of the Grecian States around him he likewise seeks a law. He applies to the best of his ability the principles of common-sense. He asks: What is the specific end of the concrete thing we call the State? What is the actual nature of the organization which we call political ? What is needed that this organization may most effectually accomplish its end?

Aristotle saw everywhere a process of growth. The very lowest form contained, potentially, the highest and best. Practically, Aristotle followed the method of evolution. If one wishes to know the end for which anything exists, he must study the concrete thing itself. States, commonwealths, communities, do not have an abstract existence in the clouds, — they are realities of this earth. Established by human beings, they contain *in posse* a final, highest, and most perfect organization. To Aristotle, the work of political science consisted in studying each political phenomenon as an unfolding of the principle of life, a manifestation of what Nature was after, a step in the ascending series to the perfect and best.

Yet such a commonwealth as the United States of America would have violated all Aristotle's canons of the essential polity of the best State. The vast extent of territory; the many races of men making up the body of citizens; the conflicting interests of the widely divided sections; the prevalence of opposite views of culture, religion, economics, domestic habits, and modes of life, — all these features would seem to him contradictory to every principle of a well-ordered civil polity, fatal to permanence, and utterly incapable of promoting the ends which a State ought to have in view as the very object of its existence; namely, the virtue, the happiness, the moral and intellectual development of all its citizens. The Greek State was everything, in fact, to the individual citizen. It supervised his household affairs, his education, his religion, and the thousand details of his daily life. Its object was to cultivate virtue, and it assigned to each citizen his work. What we leave to public opinion the Greek made the subject of law. In Aristotle's view, the statesman is the vital, spiritual power in the commonwealth; the State itself is the nurse of science and the school of philosophy, — in itself the one sufficient means for attaining a good life. The good, the perfectly rounded life is the very end for which the State exists.

What, then, is Aristotle's definition of a State? It is a whole, formed of parts which share in a common feeling, interest, and action; and this whole has been constituted for the attainment of a complete and fully developed life for all. This conception is in accordance with the ordinary Greek view, albeit nobler and more comprehensive. The Greek citizen was essentially a part of the city-State in which he was born and had his home.[1] The city laid hold of the individual to absorb his individual claims. The sphere of government in modern times has embraced chiefly the protection of life and property. Politics has thus meant little beyond practical arrangements for the punishment of crime, the defence of personal liberty, and the protection of vested interests in property. But to the Greek the State was his religion, his culture, his social club,—not merely his protector against foreign enemies and domestic injustice. He breathed and acted through the organs which the State furnished him. Beyond this corporate life, he was an exile and a vagabond. Hence, with Aristotle the State must not be too large for a common life to be lived by its citizens. The State must be a unit; and of this unit each citizen is a component part.

The State, according to the Aristotelian idea, has its origin in nature and natural relations. Nature joins together the father, the mother, the child, and the slave, who constitute a family. Several families constitute a village; many villages constitute a State, united together " at first that they may live, but continuing united together that they may live happily and well." Like every other object in the natural world, civil government is a whole, and really exists in idea before it exists in actual form. It is the inherent power of development that constitutes a particular animal: so is it with the State. The individ-

[1] The city of Boston would form a State many times larger than the largest Greek city.

ual man is not complete in himself, and he bears the same relation to the State that the individual organs bear to the entire human body.   Not to need the State as a complement to one's limited self is to be either a monster or a god.   Man perfected by society is the most excellent of all living beings; but given up to selfish appetite, he is the worst.   Therefore, as in determining the true nature of any other species we take the most perfect specimen in its highest state of development, so we should take man in his highest condition of social development, unfolding fully his noblest powers and his most humane characteristics.

How different is the theory of Rousseau, which stimulated the imagination and fired the heart of the civilized world in those days of revolutionary fervor and philosophic zeal, when civilization was represented as the curse of human society, and a return to natural conditions was considered the only way to make progress in virtue!  How different is the " Leviathan " of Hobbes, the monster from whom society had its first spring and its primal origin, — fear, that arose from mutual hate and internecine war!  In Aristotle's philosophic view, the State is the natural outgrowth of human qualities and tendencies; and it is as congenial to the nature of man to live in society as it is for the plant to send its rootlets down into the soil, its stem up into the air, and to scatter its seed on the wind.  The families of men uniting in a social union obey a divine instinct, even as the trees of the forest do when their seed is planted in congenial soil, or the honey-bees when they construct their cells. How different is the theory of an original compact which Locke enunciates as the origin of government! "The original compact, which begins and actually constitutes any political society," he says, "is nothing but the consent of any number of freemen capable of a majority to unite and to incorporate into such a society; and this is that, and that only, which could give beginning to any lawful government in the world." This theory served its purpose against the theory of the original and divine right of kings; but for real philosophical comprehension of the origin of government, Aristotle's view is infinitely superior: "As we make use of our bodily members before we understand the end and purpose of this exercise, so it is by nature itself that we are bound together and associated in political society."

Hence the State grows up naturally, man being by his very nature a political animal. As Homer says, "He that hath no tribe, or state, or home, is as solitary as a bird of prey." Man is the only animal that has reason, and so has language, which is not merely an expression of pleasure and pain, but of the just and the unjust. The impulse toward association is thus universal and natural. By carrying out this impulse in the formation of the State, man becomes the most excellent of living beings instead of the most helpless and the worst. He embodies in the State justice, which is the rule of social order.

The family, according to Aristotle, is the unit of

social life; and in it man has three relations, — husband, father, and master. Here the philosopher runs counter to our modern ideas of the injustice of slavery. He discusses the matter, indeed; for even in his day some had maintained that slavery was unjust. But Aristotle maintains that they are slaves by nature who have strength of body without ability to take care of themselves; and that to them a master is a benefit, — and not only to them, but to the community also. But the master should be as well fitted for ruling as the slave for obeying; then both will be profited. No Greek, again, should be enslaved, even if taken captive in war. This opinion was contrary to the universal custom of the age; for the entire population of Hellenic cities, when conquered, was often reduced to slavery. Aristotle further maintains that whenever a slave plainly shows himself qualified for freedom, he should be set free. Had the Stagirite lived a few generations later, he would have seen thousands of his Greek countrymen — among them men of culture and of high intelligence, scholars and philosophers — held as slaves in the households of the rude Romans, who doubtless thought that they were doing a service to the commonwealth, as well as to themselves, by keeping the effeminate Greeks closely subjected to their own stronger will and convenience. The doctrine that outsiders and barbarians can justly be enslaved would perhaps have assumed a different aspect to Aristotle, had he known that the barbarian would put his own interpretation upon the principle that might is the law of right.

But the slowness of the advance of humanity in social justice can be estimated from the fact that even Locke could write, as late as the seventeenth century, " There is another sort of servants, which by a peculiar name we call slaves, who, being captives taken in a just war, are by the rights of nature subjected to the absolute dominion and arbitrary power of their masters. These men having, as I say, forfeited their life, and with it their liberties, and lost their estates, and being in a state of slavery, not capable of any property, cannot in that state be considered as any part of civil society." [1] To Aristotle, we should remember, a slave was not an end in himself, but an instrument to carry out the purposes of his master, — a part of his master, though a separable part.

The city-state, then, is a whole, an integral unit, formed by the congregation of villages for the attainment of a complete life of virtue, and for the development of all the human activities. To discover the best organization of this whole is the work of political science. A study of the course of historical development is not the only need, for the historical process may have been warped and distorted. These distortions, as well as all the other phenomena, must be tested by the principles of ethics. The inquiry thus arises, What constitution of the State is most favorable to virtue in the citizen and to the common good? To answer this question wisely, Aristotle investigates the economical and social phenomena which result from different kinds of

[1] Locke's Works, ii. 181.

government, the character of the citizens, the features of the territory, the different ways of getting wealth; and he considers the adaptation of proposed changes to the circumstances of the people. Plato had sought to establish an ideal commonwealth, which by its very construction should be a model State, wherein all the variable elements of human nature should be constrained to harmonious adjustment. Aristotle shows what elements are necessary to make the State what it should be to accomplish its natural results. He is fully aware that the "best State" will be a rare thing in the world's history; and so he occupies himself often with practical suggestions on the reform of abuses, the remedies for evils, and the beneficial changes that may be made in actual forms of government.

The citizens of Aristotle's "best State" are those only who have undergone a special training, who have ample leisure for gymnastics, for practice in arms, and for the pursuit of philosophy and noble learning. But all those who work for pay in any industrial pursuit are excluded from the right to rule or to choose their rulers. In the democratic States of Greece the laborers and artisans were ranked as citizens, and they enjoyed equal rights as voters with the noblest and the richest. But in Sparta and some other States, where "useful and necessary work" was performed by slaves, the industrial life virtually excluded one from all liberal pursuits, such as those of the soldier, the statesman, and the philosopher. Even agriculture lay under the ban of condemnation, as it allowed only talk of crops and bullocks. The tradesman and the merchant were also regarded as pursuing sordid and mercenary trades. All useful occupations performed for pay were deemed servile and ignoble. Even the teacher of philosophy who taught for regular pay was the object of Plato's bitterest scorn. When to-day we hear the system of wages denounced by laborers as nothing but slavery, it will remind us of the advance made toward giving what Aristotle called the useful and illiberal pursuits of life a recognition in the commonweal.

Aristotle's State, as a natural whole made up of parts, is subject to the laws of every structure of a like constitution. In this whole made up of many members, some must rule and others must be ruled. There is in the State a natural inequality among the different elements. As in every object made up of parts some are only means subservient to a higher end, so it is in the State. The tools with which a house is built are no part of the house itself. Every animal has parts which are useful only for certain ancillary purposes, and these must be held strictly to their subordinate office. The lower half of the body exists for the upper; and throughout all Nature there is, as in the egg, that which is meant to grow, and that also which is meant to promote growth. The same principles apply in the State that we see rule in every living organism in the natural world. Shakspeare's social view is similar. The wise Ulysses, in "Troilus and Cressida," says: —

> " How could communities, . . .
>    But by degrees, stand in authentic place?
>    Take but degree away, untune that string,
>    And, hark, what discord follows! each thing meets
>    In mere oppugnancy. . . .
>    Strength should be lord of imbecility,
>    And the rude son should strike his father dead.
>    Force should be right. . . .
>    Then everything includes itself in power,
>    Power into will, will into appetite;
>    And appetite, a universal wolf,
>    So doubly seconded with will and power,
>    Must make, perforce, a universal prey,
>    And, last, eat up himself. "

The science of Aristotle sees the same law of order, degree, and subordinated powers and capacities in every living organism, whether in the natural or the social world. He gives the beehive as a special example in his natural history of animals. Shakspeare has put the same comparison into the mouth of the politic Archbishop of Canterbury, in "Henry V.": —

> " Therefore doth Heaven divide
>    The state of man in divers functions,
>    Setting endeavor in continual motion;
>    To which is fixed, as an aim or butt,
>    Obedience: for so work the honey-bees,
>    Creatures that by a rule in Nature teach
>    The act of order to a peopled kingdom."

No better summary than this could be given of Aristotle's best form of State organization.

To Aristotle the whole modern system of credit,

interest, monetary exchange, based upon the infinite
complexity and variety of claims involved, is wrong.
He holds that it leads to the unbounded acquisition of wealth, and causes the means of living to
be mistaken for the end. To buy and sell merely
for profit is a perversion of trade, which should
be carried on only to satisfy the needs of existence.
To make money produce money is unnatural. As
Shakspeare expresses it, to take interest is to
make barren metal breed metal. Aristotle would
have every commercial transaction a direct exchange of social services. But strange are the
standards of right and wrong, of justice and injustice, in every age! Just as his commonwealth, if it
wanted fish, could catch them from the sea; or if
it needed game, could hunt wild animals on land,
so if it lacked slaves, it could make war for them
upon some weak and alien nation. Money may
not breed money, but slaves may breed slaves!

The citizens of Aristotle's State are to have, as
far as possible, a common interest, a common aim,
and a common enjoyment of the means of education and amusement provided by the powers that
be. But he severely criticises Plato's scheme of
community of property and community of offspring.
Plato would abolish the idea of *mine* and *thine.*
To be free from the quarrels caused by property
and individual relationships, he would do away with
them altogether. Aristotle uses the same valid
arguments that we employ to-day. The difficulties
of living in harmony where there is no individual

property, he says, are very great. Where colonies
are settled with a common ownership of property,
there are continual disputes about the most trifling
matters. There are disputes also as to the labor al-
lotted and the compensation received; complaints,
criminations, and recriminations, and even blows,
abound. If all things are common, no one can
give assistance to his friend or help to the needy;
no one can be generous, no one can be grateful,
no one self-relying. If there were no individual
property, some evils would be removed, but more
evils would be brought into existence; life would
lose its zest, and unity would become a tiresome
monotony. With the development of virtue and
noble living, all the unity that is desirable will be
brought about. With community of property, industry would lack much of its present stimulus,
and not a few of the real pleasures of life would
be wanting; for many permanent and universal
tendencies of human nature would then be without
proper satisfaction.

But Aristotle, the opponent of common property,
is also opposed to the unlimited acquisition of
either wealth or land. He sees the evils of the
possession of superfluous riches, and seeks to guard
against them by the moral training of the citizens
and the limitation of buying and selling to real
exchanges of property for actual use. To accumulate for the sake of accumulation is sordid and
base, a habit unworthy of him who would live nobly and so as to benefit the State. Only those

ends are to be pursued which contribute to a full and perfect life.

Upon the relation of women to the State, Aristotle scarcely touches. Woman is a part of the household, and receives no particular consideration. Plato would emancipate her from her unnatural seclusion, and make her the equal of man in the social organization; but Aristotle looks upon her as the inferior of man, like the child and the slave: she is to form a part of the family, whose head and natural king is the husband, father, and master. Men are not to marry until they are thirty-seven years of age, or women until they are eighteen: thus there is secured for the inexperienced maiden, as far as possible, a grave and experienced counsellor and friend, and the father will not be too near of an age with the children, who should entertain for him a certain respect and reverence. But was not William von Humboldt nearer the truth, — that is, to nature and common-sense, — when he said: " The freshness of youth is the true foundation for a happy marriage. I would not for an instant say that the happiness of marriage ends with youth; but I do say that husband and wife should carry into later life the memory of years enjoyed together, if their happiness is not to lose the distinguishing characteristic of wedded bliss." Yet if Aristotle wished to make sure of the wife's silence before the husband, he certainly was wise to make the husband venerable. Comte said that the function of the household is to cultivate to the highest point the influence of woman over man; but in Aristotle's view the household is only a factor in the organization of the State which supervises it. He therefore permitted many things, such as checks against over-population, which we should consider cruel and inhuman.

On the different forms of State constitutions, which Aristotle treats at great length,[1] we need not dwell. In the small area of Hellenic territory all kinds of government were to be found, and the cities often changed rapidly from one form to another. Aristotle himself prefers the rule of one royal head, if that head be gifted with a true genius for ruling, and endowed with all the virtues that will serve to make the happiness of the people the sole end in view. But how can such a phœnix be assured? Next to such a rare and almost impossible phenomenon, the best government is a true aristocracy, — a government of the best, selected from a body of citizens instructed in the art of ruling; men of education and experience. A democracy is to Aristotle the worst form of government. This was natural, as there was no place in his scheme for the education of the great body of the people.

This vast American democracy of ours, — this graded system of town, city, county, State, and nation, — presents a grand whole, with such a subordination and combination of parts that Aristotle's provisions for attaining political ends seem insig-

[1] His exposition of the Constitution of Athens has been the latest discovery to interest the learned world.

nificant in comparison. To-day the sex he set aside as not capable of citizenship presses forward for complete recognition; and many women labor zealously for a State looking to the highest good of all the people, and administered by all the people. Aristotle feared a State too large and a people too numerous. He did not dream that vast diversity of interests, infinite variety of productions, complexity of institutions, opposite systems of religion, varied soil and climate, different ideals held by many classes of society, and employments and methods of living endlessly varied, — that all these could work together to secure permanence and stability in the constitution of the State.

Yet if we look at the American situation in another light, the remotest parts of our country are not much farther apart than were the remotest cities of Greece, thanks to the railway, the telephone, and the telegraph. Moreover, the means of education have in our case been infinitely multiplied in schools, churches, and the products of the printing-press. But though thus aided by invention and by wide-spread knowledge in preserving alive an enormous State, we have — even more than the Greeks had — to rely on intelligence, courage, and faith to overcome the difficulties that confront us.

At the present time we have followers of Aristotle and followers of Plato, — men who unconsciously range themselves among the scientific

students of natural and social phenomena, and
men who construct castles in the air, cities in
the clouds, and believe in Utopian ideals, the
more fervently the more impracticable they appear.  Plato depreciated natural science and the
study of physical objects, giving it credit only as
a pleasant pastime, " a means of pleasure which
did not bring repentance with it."  This world
was but the spring-board from which the soul
was to make its bound into the infinite, the permanent, the ideal, the divine.  He knew nothing of
our modern reverent study of Nature; for in natural existences was the cause of all evil, and the realm
of ideas was to him the only realm of reality.  The
temporary and changing phenomena of life he
deemed unworthy of philosophic thought, and the
real statesman was he who could discern essential
causes, and see what was, in itself and eternally,
noble and just.  Philosophers, or men of insight
into divine realities, were of necessity the rulers in
Plato's ideal commonwealth.

The method of the " Politics " was just the opposite from this; for Aristotle reverenced the facts of
Nature, and from these unfolded the general law.
Plato, starting from the realm of ideas, looked upon
every object of sense as a declension from the divine
order, as a loss of reality, an immersion in the
world of matter and of sense, a descent from eternal and permanent goodness and truth.  To study
the actual development of institutions, and from
various forms of existing States to deduce the

laws of political science, was entirely counter to his method of philosophizing. All past and present State-institutions were monstrous and abnormal phenomena, violations of the divine ideas of righteousness and justice, and at the best could be only warnings, — buoys as it were, to show the limits of the channel or the sunken reefs. The "Politics," on the contrary, has for its main thesis the identification of the State and individual well-being. The end for which man exists is not in himself, but in that city-State of which he makes a part. As in the animal every member and limb is subordinate to the organization as a whole, and as the plan of this whole gives the normal status or form which each and every part must assume, — so in the social organism, or State, the good or well-being of the whole constitutes the norm, or rule, to which every individual part must conform itself, if there is to be the highest development. And with Aristotle this may be said to constitute the absolute ethics; namely, the identification of the individual with the State.

This would seem, then, to be no new doctrine; yet this is claimed as something peculiar to the modern development of socialistic theories. I turn to a book called the " Ethics of Socialism," and there I read the following : —

" At last, with the dawn of a new economic era, — the era of social production for social uses, — we shall have also the dawn of a new Ethic ; an Ethic whose ideal is neither personal holiness nor personal interest, but social happiness, for which the perfect individual will ever be subordinate to the perfect society. The test of personal character will here be the possession of social qualities and the zeal for positive and definite social ends. This may be termed in a sense an absolute Ethic. In this new conception of duty the individual consciously subordinates himself to the community. The separation of ethics from politics, and of both from religion, is finally abolished. In socialism, ethics become political, and politics become ethical; while religion means but the higher and more far-reaching aspect of that ethical sense of obligation, duty, fraternity, which is the ultimate bond of every-day society."

Could a better statement be made of Aristotle's view of the end and aim of social organization? It adds nothing to it. To be sure, Aristotle had a different view of what constitutes fraternity; but this does not affect the moral purpose and the philosophic groundwork of his social and political theory.

This, then, is the *new* Ethic, this the supreme and satisfying ideal for which humanity is to work! The struggles of the human heart for these two thousand years; the aspirations for a divine life and for a destiny beyond time and sense; the vision of immortality; the communion with the great and good of all ages; the rising into higher states of loving, disinterested service; the opening vistas of progressive knowledge, and of unfolding states and modes of being, — all this is to be abolished, and that which constitutes "the bond of every-day society " is to be the embodiment of all striving, the all-sufficient aim of the denizens of this wonderful universe! Aristotle expressed the highest conception of that Greek civilization; but there is now a higher; and this higher conception is not abandoned, though it may seem lost in the transition from a lower to a higher form. "Attacks on religion," as Benjamin Constant well says, " do not mean that mankind is ready to say good-by to religion, but simply that its popular forms no longer fit the needs of the souls which have outgrown them and desire something purer and larger."

There is a higher view of man in his political and social destiny than either Plato or Aristotle saw, — a commonwealth of humanity whose foundation is in the earth, but whose superstructure is in the realm of eternal and spiritual ideas; and we are made citizens of that commonwealth, not by any written constitution or any geographical boundaries, but by oneness of spirit, and by sympathy with every effort for the well-being of man.

# X.

## SOCIAL PROGRESS.

PROGRESS in the animal world consists in manifestation of more highly organized forms of life, from the simplest cell to the most wonderful and compact human brain. Social progress is the advance from the wandering savage, sufficient for his own few individual needs, to the citizen of to-day, dependent every moment on the ministration of his fellows in a thousand ways for comfort and even life. At every stage we see that society becomes a more highly organized form of life, each part more dependent, each nerve more sensitive, each remotest organ more fully ministrant to the needs and well-being of the whole, — from the bald monotony of the old village community, to the boiling stir and lively commotion of the country of the telegraph, the railway, and the daily newspaper.

This social progress has been in the direction of the organization of industry, the application of mind to all the various employments, occupations, and comforts of life. Where all work is performed by slaves, what object in lessening their toils, or making efforts to increase their leisure? The wisest of the ancients could see no other way than the slavery

of the many in order that the few might have leisure for culture and the means of citizenship. The
slow centuries have evolved the true idea of manhood, and on it, as on an eternal foundation, rests
our social as well as our political superstructure.

The wonderful simplicity of those arrangements
by which human progress is promoted escapes our
notice, and therefore it may be well to look more
minutely at what takes place every moment, and is
more truly miraculous than if man's food were
brought to him every day and laid at his feet by
some fowl of the air or some beast of the field. No
delicate piece of machinery ever devised by man is
so delicate, so complex, so intricately involved in
its parts as this living machine which we call society, the body politic, the social organization, the
modern democratic State.

How are such results secured as we witness every
moment, and secured so universally that we do not
take thought of them, any more than we do of our
breathing, of our walking, of our ordinary use of
speech? Think how many innumerable services
are combined in order to clothe any average citizen
of the millions of our people! The cotton, silk,
flax, wool, and leather, coming from every quarter
of the world, have passed through how many hands,
how many changes, how many processes of production, manufacture, and distribution! The imagination flags before this infinite complexity of labors,
inventions, industries, and trades. Look upon a
table set out for the commonest meal, and reflect

what generations of men have conspired to clear, defend, and till the land; to plant, reap, grind, and prepare the grain; how many men have delved in mines, how many labored to perfect machines; and what forces of air, water, and steam have been brought into play before that simple loaf of bread was placed upon the table; — take in all this, and pass over then as commonplace and insignificant, if you can, that wonderful system of social arrangements by which, for a trifle on your part, you can be put into possession not only of that loaf of bread, but of a vast variety of products which by your own individual efforts you never could have earned in thousands of years, though you had a hundred contriving heads and a hundred skilful hands. It is the conspiring labor of the human race that has built our houses, ordained justice, established schools, and secured the means of material, intellectual, and spiritual good, — more, infinitely more, than the wisest, the strongest, could ever obtain by his own individual labor and skill. Yet each one, by doing his daily work, becomes a share-holder in this vast company. With his day's work he pays his part of the debt to the human race. Is there no harmonious working in the laws by which so wonderful a result is brought about?

Reflect what a triumph of commissariat ability is involved in supplying a few hundred soldiers with what is necessary to eat and drink for a few days. Still more, consider how the supplies of every town and city seem to take care of themselves. Four millions of people in London are daily fed, and what organized corps of planners, what human foresight and supervision, could accomplish this result which comes so easily and so regularly from so many channels, and with such incredible labors by land and by sea, by lane and by highway, by railroad and by river! And each one is benefited in the same ratio of an infinity of services from others over and above what he himself can furnish. Is there not something wonderful in that system of economic laws by which society is established and kept together, — by which services are rendered, exchanges effected, and needed products furnished for the social well-being of the race? Is this equilibrium of forces, this calling forth of efforts, this restraining of excesses, this remedying of deficiencies, this universal supplying of needs, — is this a trifling affair?

Each man's labor does seem so small an affair! He ploughs a few acres, cuts a few soles or uppers, fashions a few pin-heads or points, digs a little lead or iron or coal out of the rock, enters a few figures in a ledger, drives a few nails, sets up a few types, — and what does his work amount to? If he look at the sum-total of that alone, reckoned up in its solitary bigness, he feels small enough. But it does not stand alone; it has relations with every other man's work, and every other man's work with it. It is an essential part of the grand result; it gives him a share in the work of all other men. The race is at work to supply each one's special need. A traveller once said of London, that " he believed if you

had a hole between the third and fourth upper molar
of the left jaw, and had reason to think that a tooth-
pick of nickel cut with cycloidal lines, and curved
on the pattern of the lines of the pillars of the Par-
thenon, was necessary for it, and went into a tooth-
pick shop and asked for it, you would find that that
particular thing had been provided for an emer-
gency just like yours, and that a stock was kept
with a view to future necessities."

You then are at work to supply some want; and
your neighbor, if he is an honest man, is also at
work to supply your want and that of other people
besides. Show your title to any service, and you
can get it. What is this title or certificate? Money.
A dollar, say, stands for so much service to be rendered to you by the human race; it stands for so
much service of a particular kind rendered by *you*,
if you worked for it, — by your ancestors, if you inherited it. You have this ticket: what will you take
it out in? One man in land, another in books;
one in a house, another in fancy goods of various
kinds; one in eatables, another in drinkables, — until
the ticket is punched out in all its values. One
man says, perhaps, "I will not present my certificate just now; I will postpone it for a month or a
year. You, neighbor, may use it, and get such service as you can out of it, paying me so much for
using it, just as you would pay me for using my
horse or my wagon or my house; only, be sure
that I get it back again at the end of the time."

A dollar, then, is the record of so much service

rendered, and is the title to so much service to be rendered in return. You may hoard it up or use it up, loan it or throw it away; you may spend it yourself, or give it to posterity: so far as it goes, it is a good title to all the manifold labors of all mankind. Thus, every blow with the hammer, every stroke with the pen, every stitch with the needle, every throw of the shuttle, every revolving of the wheel, is one more bond of union of the part with the whole, in this vast aggregate of human services that constitutes what we call "civilization" or "social development."

And without some feeling that what he does is of some use, — that is, has a relation to the great fabric of human weal, — no man can be content with his life, no man can receive true joy from his work. But a perception of this relation gives elasticity to the muscle, light to the eye, cheer to the spirit, and speed to the weary hour of toil. The humblest worker may truly say, " I also help raise the great edifice of society and of social well-being."

Many a man becomes discouraged, loses heart, sinks into listlessness, or throws himself into the whirl of dissipated folly, because he fails to recognize how infinitely great is the least effort in its relation to the whole, and how infinitely small is the most gigantic strength when isolated and separate from the social mass of benefit. There is a world of meaning in that old story of the poor Yankee and the wealthy Pennsylvania Quaker, when the former applied to the latter for help in his need.

"Friend," said the Quaker, "I will furnish thee with work, and pay thee for it; but it is not my custom to give alms to one able to labor like thee."

"That's just what I want," replied the other; "I am willing to work."

"Well," said the Quaker, "there is a log yonder, and here is an axe. Thee may pound on that log with the head of the axe; and if thee is diligent and faithful, I will pay thee a dollar a day."

"I'd as soon do that as anything else," said the laborer; and accordingly he pounded and pounded on the log with the head of the axe. After a while his energies began to flag, and in half an hour, coming to a full stop, he threw away the axe, saying, "I'll be hanged if I'll cut wood without seeing the chips fly."

Good for the poor fellow! He wanted to effect some end, to feel that he was doing something more than earning his dollar. No one of us is content to pound merely for the sake of pounding. Said Dr. Channing, more than fifty years ago, —

"To get a living a man must be useful. It is strange that laboring men do not think more of the vast usefulness of their toils, and take a benevolent pleasure in them on this account. This beautiful city, with its houses, furniture, markets, public walks, and numberless accommodations, has grown up under the hands of artisans and other laborers; and ought they not to take a disinterested joy in their work? One would think that a carpenter or mason, on passing a house which he had helped to rear, would say to himself, 'This work of mine is giving comfort

and enjoyment every day and hour, and will continue
to be a kindly shelter, a domestic gathering-place, an
abode of affection after I sleep in the dust;' and
ought not a generous satisfaction to spring up at the
thought?"

Must we wait for a new organization of society to
feel this satisfaction? It may belong to the hod-
carrier, to the hewer of wood and to the ham-
merer of stone, as well as to the architect or to the
skilled mechanic. Having this in mind, I was surprised to read the words of another Boston clergyman, the other day, when he said that no man could
derive satisfaction from mere manual labor, but only
from skilled work. It is a fact of social progress,
indeed, that more and more the great forces of Nature are brought to do the muscular drudgery of the
world; but can this drudgery be entirely eliminated?
Cannot there be for the laborer, as well as for the
artist, a noble consolation and an ideal outlook?

The law of social development is as simple as it
is universal. The basis of all movement is a human want; and in order to satisfy this want, labor
is requisite. At first, man has only his own hands
with which to work; but he invents tools, — the
pick, the plough, the wheel, the axe, etc., — and
thus the gratuitous and mighty forces of Nature are
turned into his service and made to do his bidding.
Every new application of these forces inures to the
benefit of man universally, — not merely of the particular man who invents the machine, or of him who
applies it to use. The capitalist gains much less

relative advantage from improvements in machinery than the community at large. Every conquest over natural powers, every new servant of the brain brought to do man's bidding, takes so much from the cost of what is intended to supply some human want. The labor of the hands, at every step of mechanical improvement, at every employment of natural forces, — such as gravitation, heat, attraction, in air, water, vapor, and gas, — becomes proportionally less and less, while Nature supplies more and more of her invisible ministrants. For these helpers no charge is made. Only open a way for Nature to serve, and she runs to do your bidding. She asks nothing but to have the way kept free for service. Keep that in good condition, and she neither strikes, nor asks tor higher pay, nor even quits work when the sun goes down. She will not be bound apprentice to any one exclusive master. Does the inventor nod, she serves some one who is wide awake. Does he appropriate too much to his own benefit, a hundred rivals start up where there is an open field for work, and immediately some simpler process is invented, some better machine, some cheaper method; and thus there is the unfailing tendency to benefit the whole, — for more of the gain that comes from the employment of these untiring, unreasoning, ever-obedient slaves passes over to the credit of the many than to that of the few.

The houses of a few large land-owners were once the only abodes of even a modicum of comfort, the sole possessors of many books, of fine furniture, of works of luxury and art. But even these few would look with wonder upon the accumulated resources and means belonging to thousands and tens of thousands of average citizens to-day. Once the king's courier could travel, perhaps, at great trouble and expense, two hundred miles a day; now the laborer, at the cost of an hour's work, can send his courier a thousand miles in a few minutes of time. Kings now must travel upon the people's iron highway, if they would travel as fast as the people themselves; the books read by the rich are no longer a few illuminated manuscripts, purchased at an incredible cost because made entirely by human labor; but they are printed and bound by machinery, and so are within the reach of all. Thus the relative gain of the community of men, at every step of social development through economic law, is vastly greater than the gain of the capitalist, or of the few pampered possessors of exclusive claims to lordship and privilege and superfluous wealth. The average level is continually rising, and the number of sharers in any common application of natural forces grows larger every day.

Now, because of the helping forces of Nature wealth increases; and this wealth, over and above what is immediately used, is the measure of man's triumph over Nature, as well as of Nature's gratuitous service in the supply of human wants. What is property, then? It is the symbol of power over Nature; or, rather, it is the record and the expression of the use which man has made of the forces of the material universe. It is the result of so much work done; and if you will, you can exchange your share for so much work of a different kind. Says a writer on the " Political Life of our Time, —

" Where Nature does everything for man, and man can live from hand to mouth, capital has no increase and society no progress. Capital and civilization have gone hand in hand. The results of a man's isolated contests with the difficulties of Nature are extremely limited, but all-powerful and productive in the accumulated effort of the race. This constitutes the real fixed capital of our time, existing not only in our material riches, — buildings and machinery, — but in the experience, the foresight, and the prudence embodied in the agriculture, trades, and letters of the day.

Because it is of so much vital significance, property has been the great object which all government and all organized forms of order have sought to secure and to protect. Without this safety and security, man remains a savage and a brute. He even sinks below the level of the brute. The brute does not know what property is : it has properties, — that is, faculties, — exactly proportioned to its limited needs. Its faculties, or properties, are good for just so much and no more, — for the secretion of so much honey or wax or web; for the obtaining of so much food; for the construction of a shelter on just such a pattern; for the living in just such an environment : in a word, the wants, and the properties by which it supplies those wants, are nicely correlated, exactly measured, the one by the other. But it is the prerogative of man to have *property*, — that is, an accumulation of material things beyond the satisfaction of his own immediate wants. While animals of one species have precisely the same wants and the same properties, man has infinitely various wants to be supplied in infinitely various ways; man has a personality not identical with the properties of his nature; he has a spiritual force not measured by his beak, his claws, or his teeth. Now, the symbol of this personality, this force, is property, — that is, something over and above man's purely physical necessities, his wants of the moment; something which represents the services he may claim of his fellow-men, according to the estimate set by the community at any given time; something which entitles him to so many supplies to the wants of body, mind, or taste, — clothing, books, houses, pictures, fields; services of all kinds except the spontaneous affections of the heart. Here is a plane above the operation of the economic laws; here is the kingdom not of this world. Character, moral worth, is the reality, while property is only a symbol.

But because property is such a weighty symbol, it has always possessed a mysterious power; it represents so much force, so much industry, so much excellence, so much self-restraint, so much forethought somewhere and in some souls, but not necessarily in those particular persons who may possess it at the present moment. Thus property carries with

it a prestige, indefinable, subtile, universally pene-
trating; so that he who does not feel it, and is not
unconsciously swayed by it, has been pronounced
" a miracle in Nature." But this prestige is not an
unmixed evil: it is one of those appearances by
which man is lured on to his higher destiny. He
is trained and educated through symbols, and pri-
marily through the world of Nature, which is itself
only a symbol.

See the operation of the universal law. Man
attains a sense of personality, a feeling of pure,
spiritual activity so far as he rules, directs, and masters the natural world. Just so far as he subdues
and possesses Nature, just so far does he come into
the knowledge, the use, and the enjoyment of his
own faculties as a spiritual being. The savage, who
uses Nature as coextensive only with the supply of
his pressing animal needs from day to day, remains
stationary, makes little social progress, attains no
high degree of social development. He looks upon
the forces of Nature as cruel and relentless foes; he
sees in lightning and in torrent only wrathful ministers
of vengeance. He feels his own weakness, his own
subjection, his own wretchedness. Nature is not to
him a mirror in which his own powers are reflected,
a standard by which his own strength is measured;
but it is a crushing tyrant, before whom he must
unconditionally yield.

But every advance made by man in subduing
Nature demonstrates his power and measures his
essential worth. He accumulates more than he

uses for his present wants; and that accumulation is his capital. *That* symbolizes his power and his greatness; *that* moves him from place to place, unfolds to him the secrets of the stars, opens to him the glories of the past, sends his messages with lightning swiftness, turns the swamp into a garden, fills his ear with music and his house with the means of comfort and of ease; *that* sets in motion multitudes of men, and makes his word almost omnipotent in the material world.

Thus social progress is the result of man's rule over Nature's powers, of his activity in the supply of various human wants. And the symbol of this power, the representative of this essential prerogative of man — property — has been instinctively and blindly pursued as if it were the real and only good in itself. The idol has been worshipped as if it were the god. In this material sheath the higher spiritual development of man has been cared for and protected; for in its building up of material interests humanity is building up something better than it now sees. Through the free and unrestricted operation of the laws inherent in life and the world, the great problems of society will have their solution. The special organization is beyond the device of any individual skill; but the time will come when the general means of good shall so far surpass any one man's peculiar appropriation, that the idol shall be dashed in pieces, and the domain of Nature pass entirely over to man. At every step of the transfer, what are now exclusive benefits will then be distributed as a common heritage. The privileges of the few in learning and art are rapidly becoming the possibilities of all. The general level of comfort, of opportunity, of knowledge, is rising from year to year; and to doubt of the sufficiency of the in-working laws of humanity for evolving the highest good is to doubt the splendid achievements of the present and the no less splendid possibilities of the future.

"Man ought never to be troubled about the means of subsistence," says the Hindu apologue in its admirable simplicity; "for *that* the Creator provides. A mother has no sooner given birth to her child, than two fountains of milk flow from the maternal bosom." This suggests a truth which every stage of human progress does but make more plain. In it are volumes of social science; in it is the prophecy of everything relating to moral and natural subsistence. Every supply which humanity needs comes in its time; every child of inventive genius opens the sealed fountains of Nature's maternal breast. To be alarmed lest iron and coal and oil shall fail! Let them fail: there is water, there is air, there is sunlight to render up their infinite stores of good.

What is the lesson taught over and over again? Whenever the old has ceased, some better new has taken its place; whenever the old faith and the old form are but husks, behold! from the unknown depth of the human spirit comes some fresh inspiration, some renewing ideal. When the wider field and the virgin soil were needed for the seed of a more perfect manhood, the compass was made known, and bold heart and seeing mind sailed forth into unknown seas. And so each generation is supplied out of an infinite fountain of good, each day giving some new application of the forces of the natural world to man's physical, social, and spiritual exigencies. We need to see, then, the eternal laws of order, of harmony, of universal tendency to good shining in the firmament above, however dark may be the night, and however hidden may be the road. A great social theorist of the past generation, Leroux, interpreted aright the lesson that is taught to us all, when we look with upward gaze into the heavens over our heads, and let " the soul of things " speak to our hearts. He says : —

" Last evening, as I walked, I was thinking upon the ills that afflict humanity, the ignorance and the passion that oppose its progress ; upon how hard it is to spread abroad a new idea, and how the truths most essential to man's happiness and well-being are ignored and persecuted ; and thus thinking, I became sad and discouraged. Suddenly I lifted up my eyes : the stars were shining in the heavens. I had gazed only a moment, when a voice within me said : ' Thou who thus art afflicted at the woes of humanity, and would 'st have them removed in one single instant, look at those stars, and remember that not centuries, but millions upon millions of centuries are needed for their light to reach the eye and show their

place in the heavens.' With this thought, peace and hope
entered my soul, and my moral sanity was restored."

Neither must we be misled by shooting stars or
sparkling meteors that flash across the sky. It is
related of President Lincoln, " that in the gloomiest
period of the war he had a call from a large delega-
tion of bank presidents. One of them asked him
whether his confidence in the permanency of the
Union was not beginning to be shaken; to which
this embodied genius of common-sense made the
following reply: ' Gentlemen, when I was a young
man in Illinois, I boarded for a time with a worthy
deacon of the Presbyterian Church. One night I
was roused from my sleep by a rap at the door, and
I heard the deacon's voice exclaiming, " Get up,
Abraham ! the day of judgment has come ! " Springing from the bed I rushed to the window, and saw
great showers of falling stars; but looking back of
them, I saw in the heavens the grand old constella-
tions fixed and true in their well-known places.
Gentlemen,' he added, ' the world did not come to
an end then, nor will the Union now.' "

The great social result we now see has been
brought about without any one man's, or all men's,
direct or voluntary contrivance, — a result plastic to
every higher, in-pressing tendency. May we not
say, then, in regard to social development what an
eminent physiologist[1] says in regard to the physical
universe, that " to see a great result brought about

[1] Nature and Man.   By W. B. Carpenter.   P. 382.

by the consentaneous but diversified action of a
multitude of individuals, each of whom does his
own particular work in a manner that combines
harmoniously with the different work of every other,
suggests to me nothing but admiration for the
Master-mind by which that order was devised."

## XI.

## SOCIAL PLANS AND PROBLEMS.

IN his grandest Ode, — "Intimations of Immortality from the Recollections of Early Childhood," — Wordsworth draws, not proofs, but suggestions of man's capacity for the immortal life; and he raises the song of thanks and praise, not for the delight and liberty and hope of childhood's years, —

> " But for those obstinate questionings
> Of sense and outward things;
> Fallings from us, vanishings;
> Blank misgivings of a creature
> Moving about in worlds not realized;
> High instincts, before which our mortal nature
> Did tremble like a guilty thing surprised:
> But for those first affections,
> Those shadowy recollections,
> Which, be they what they may,
> Are yet the fountain-light of all our day,
> Are yet a master-light of all our seeing."

Equally suggestive are those dreams of a nobler than the present life, which, whether they take the form of a paradise in the ages long past, or a paradise in the coming ages of the future of humanity, alike give intimations of an immortal spirit and an eternal destiny. Man is not content with that which the eye can see and the hand can touch; in a moment, his thought travels to a fairer land and a more joyous clime.

All ages have their Utopias, their visions of republics and cities of God, their purer State and nobler organization, wherein justice shall reign and love shall rule, and all shall be sharers in a blessedness which the human heart has never truly imagined. Take away this ideal element, and few would be found to trouble themselves with plans and problems for the social good of the race. Even man's most material heaven is a protest against the limitations of time and sense. Any project or plan which has not in it something of this higher tendency, this appeal to what is noblest and best, gains no hold, or soon sinks into decay and nothingness. There is this essential greatness in humanity, — that the only cement which does not crumble, even as it is being put on, is that which has, or seems to have, a divine quality, a potency derived from its being mixed with man's purest loves and grandest aspirations. Before he has developed his capacities, before he finds out that he is capable of an infinite progress, man suffering under the evils and limitations of the present looks back to the past, whose frowning features he has forgotten, and places there his ideal state of blessedness, when he lived in innocence and peace, when the earth yielded spontaneously its stores of good, and a golden age was the heritage of the race. But the occult wisdom of the Greek mysteries and traditions taught Æschylus better than this; and he makes the beginnings of humanity in the lowest depths of ignorance and want, without the knowledge even of fire, dwelling —

> " In hollowed holes, like swarms of tiny ants,
>   In sunless depths of caverns."

It is evident that Æschylus conceived civilization as growth.

The early priesthoods were the select brotherhoods, which, withdrawn into themselves, had possession of whatever knowledge then existed, and kept it too as their own exclusive right.  In their view the multitude were to be led, and to be let into only so much acquaintance with the ancient traditions and the higher wisdom as seemed safe to the few dwellers in the inmost circle.  Among the freedom-loving Greeks, however, the exclusive lines drawn by the sacred fraternities were soon overleaped, and in the tragedies of the poets and the philosophies of the early schools was embodied whatever was vital in the mysteries and the sacerdotal fraternities.  But philosophy did not outgrow the idea of something select to be followed only by the few, who constituted a separate caste, and whose life was not to be stained by contact with the ordinary cares and business of the many.  The great philosopher Pythagoras, who preceded Plato, and to whom Plato was vastly indebted, founded a secret society, or religious community, into whose mystic wisdom only those were admitted who underwent years of initiatory preparation by silence, by prayer, by purify-

ing services, until they were deemed worthy to receive the knowledge of the inmost revelations of
science and religion. The discipline which Pathag-
oras instituted was intended to raise up a company
of select souls, who should be the teachers of mankind, and who should live a separate and divine life.
It was a new method of living, and his disciples received a training in science, in morals, and in political knowledge. It was their mingling in politics,
together with their aristocratic bearing and haughty
exclusiveness, which brought about their destruction
as an order and scattered them over Greece. It is
easy for us to comprehend how that which holds
others in contempt should itself finally become the
victim of contempt in other men.

In all ages religion appears to have been the consecrating bond that has kept together those who
would separate themselves from ordinary society, and
thus attain a position of freedom from its claims and
its cares. No plan of material utility alone, of sensual pleasure, of pecuniary gain, has been able to
unite for any length of time the sons and daughters
of this dreaming, aspiring human race. But some
common, infinite hope; some longing for good unbounded by the narrow limits of earth and sense, —
this has melted away the differences of external condition, of strength, of capacity, of wealth, and of outward form, and given a long lease of perpetuity to
many social arrangements. Witness the Essenes in
Egypt and Palestine; the monastic orders of the
Middle Ages; the Moravians and Shakers of modern

times.   In the earliest days of overflowing common
affection and devotion, the followers of Christ made
common cause for mutual support, and no longer
said *mine* and *thine*, as far as fellow-believers were
concerned.   But this was no association taking in
all the world; it was a solidarity among those
only who felt as brothers, and owned one common
head; it was a passing, temporary condition of
things, as limited and as exclusive as the life-school
of Pythagoras, or the brotherhood of the Knights
of Saint John.

But as we travel down the ages we come into a
different atmosphere.   Individual liberty begins to
claim its rights.   Religion, more and more relegated
to a future world, ceases to regulate and preside over
the present.   Science makes known its wonderful
secrets; freedom in the sphere of politics, of thought,
and of labor makes its demands.   The American
Revolution is an object-lesson that startles the dull-
est pupil in the school of privilege and divine right.
The French Revolution, so quickly consumed by its
own excesses, scatters everywhere glowing embers,
which kindle into a living flame, and burn on and
on wherever there is wrong to be redressed and
inequalities to be removed.   The foundations up-
heaved, trembling, do not fall back again into the
old places.   "We are here," say the laboring millions,
"and we are men who claim our rights ! "

In the first quarter of the present century the voice
that gives utterance, embodying in articulate, syste-
matic tones this cry of labor, is that of the Count

Saint-Simon, who died in poverty and isolation in 1825; but not before he had given to the world his plan for the amelioration of the moral, intellectual, and physical condition of the most numerous and poorest class of modern society. He would have the State become an association of laborers, with its chosen chiefs, who should organize every department and distribute to each one his work; the present system of competition and individual rivalry and warfare should cease, and each individual labor for the good of the whole. He would have the directors of labor, the chiefs of industry, chosen by those who are most interested in the success of the association, and they should regulate all business affairs and all employments now left to chance and isolated proprietors.

"Society," he says, "is the owner of all instruments of production; it should preside over all material occupations; it can alone watch over every part of the great industrial workshop, carry means and instruments where they are needed, and, in one word, bring production into harmony with consumption. Thus will disappear the misfortunes, the reverses, the failures, to which every laborer is now exposed; industry is organized, everything is foreseen and provided for; division of labor is perfected, and the combination of all efforts becomes more potent every day."

But Saint-Simon's was only one among many enthusiastic utterances and hopeful social plans. At last, in France, the vast number of converging rays centred in one burning focus, and, as the result,

Louis Philippe in 1848 was driven from the throne. What an era was that of grandest enthusiasm and hope! The governor of Massachusetts, George N. Briggs, in his Thanksgiving proclamation exhorted us all to pray to " Our Father in Heaven, that He will vouchsafe His aid to our fellow-men in the Old World, who are struggling to throw off the oppression of ages, and to regain their long-lost rights."

The element which predominated in the early stages of this movement in France was that which the exiled king had opposed and persecuted. It was thus formulated in the defence of some republicans who were accused of violating the law by seditious utterances in 1833, three years after Louis Philippe had been made king.

" We demand," boldly said the defendants' counsel, " that labor shall no longer be made subordinate to the interests of the greedy and the idle ; that the workingman be no longer made the helpless drudge of the capitalist ; that the labor of his hands be not the sole source of profit ; that he may find in the establishment of public banks, in the diffusion of instruction, in the wise administration of justice, in the multiplication of the means of inter-communication, and in the strength of association itself, the way of enlightening his tasks, of freeing his capacities, and of recompensing his industry and courage."

It was the energy imparted by this social element that won the victory over the royal government; it was the hope which this gave that inspired the clamorous democracy and restrained their fierce excesses. Thus France stood in the vanguard of the nations, and pointed out the way in which, it was claimed, the hosts of the future must march.

Ah, well, the revolution failed; but the enthusiasm of humanity never dies!

The present socialistic atmosphere has been the gradual accretion of nearly a century of growth in democratic ideas. From 1825 to 1850 — the second quarter of our present century — was a period of social experiments under various names of communities, phalanxes, associations, unions, co-operative societies, etc., the professed object of which was to furnish a catholicon, or universal remedy, for all the ills that afflict the social body. There were between forty and fifty of these societies, with a membership of about nine thousand persons, and with an average life of less than two years. The story of these attempts to heal the sickness of society by a universal remedy is one of the most pathetic pages of human history. It is a most moving tragedy, if the essence of tragedy be the collision of the ideal and the actual, — the shipwreck of hope, aspiration, and faith, when nothing had been looked for but clear skies, favoring winds, and an open sea.

But Nature and life are inexorable. To mean well is not enough; good intentions will not make up for the want of conformity to the simple laws of intelligence, industry, patience, and order. Robert Owen, a sincere philanthropist, one of the earliest social reformers, obeyed these laws in his dealings with wood, stone, wool, and iron, and became a wealthy magnate in the manufacturing world. He disobeyed them in his philanthropic socialism, because he was ignorant of the finer qualities of individual and collective humanity. Each man is a more subtile mechanism than was ever embodied in wood or iron; and yet how easy a thing, many think, he is to put into some associate phalanstery, and how sure he is to go right! In 1824, Owen bought out the land and buildings of the Rappites on the banks of the Wabash, and issued his invitation to all the peoples of the earth to throw off the monstrous evils to which up to that hour man had been a slave. On the 4th of July, 1826, he delivered his new declaration of independence, in a hall at New Harmony, to the nine hundred souls who had been attracted by his picture of the golden opportunity to attain all human goods, without any accompanying mortal ill. He said: —

" For nearly forty years have I been employed, heart and soul, day by day, almost without ceasing, in preparing the means and arranging the circumstances to enable me to give the death-blow to the tyranny which for unnumbered ages has held the human mind spellbound in chains of such mysterious forms that no mortal has dared approach to set the suffering prisoner free ! Nor has the fulness of time for the accomplishment of this great event been completed until within this hour. Such has been the extraordinary course of events, that the Declaration of Political Independence in 1776 has produced its counterpart, the Declaration of Mental Independence in 1826, — the latter just half a century from the former."

Here certainly is self-confidence, if nothing else. But in one year from that time the bubble had burst; Mr. Owen went back to Scotland, and his poor followers went back to the beggarly elements of the outside world. A visitor to New Harmony, fifteen years afterward, was cautioned not to speak of socialism, "as the subject was unpopular." That is not very strange. Poor man! he found that men were, many of them, intractable, dishonest, lovers of liquor, lovers of their own selfish pleasure, envious, wasteful, and quarrelsome. But he never saw that a man carried himself with him wherever he went; that fine feathers did not necessarily make fine birds. He held fast to his main principle, that, put men in good circumstances, and they will necessarily be good. Ah, how easy it would be to reform the world if only the external surroundings had to be considered! But unfortunately there is such a thing as human nature in every human being; and this human nature has a trick of throwing down every obstacle, and flying, if need be, over every wall.

How often we forget this, in our impatient zeal to accomplish at one stroke what the thousand and tens of thousand ages of the slowly growing past have not yet brought about! Yes, our temple shall be constructed at once; its massive walls and graceful dome shall bless the sight now, even of this present generation. But where are the polished bricks, the hammered and jointed stones? Alas for the necessity to have the clay well burnt, rightly hardened, and deftly smoothed, and the stones, something else than crumbling pudding-stone!

When Robert Owen was seventy-five years old he again visited this country on a lecture tour, to advocate his philanthropic schemes. He was not shaken in his firm faith of being able to establish, as Adin Ballou says of him, " a great model of the new social State, which would bring the human race into a terrestrial paradise." In 1846 he lectured in the New York Assembly chamber before the delegates to form a new Constitution for that State, in which he said: —

" All religious systems, constitutions, governments, and laws are, and have been, founded in error; and that error is, that man forms his own character. They [the delegates] were about to form another Constitution based upon that error, and ere long more Constitutions would have to be made and altered, — and so on, until the truth that the character of man is formed for him shall be recognized, and the system of society based upon that principle become national and universal."

This is, expressed or unexpressed, the essential point of view, the fundamental creed, of all socialistic schemes. Louis Blanc stated it plainly in his programme, when he said: "It is not the man who is responsible for his wrong-doings, but society; and, hence, a society on a good basis will make the individual man good." With a certain class of minds there is this conviction, that external conditions are the all-important thing;

that with changed circumstances, the entire inner being will be changed. This was the expressed creed, as we have seen, of Robert Owen; and he based upon this theoretical view of man's nature all his reasonings and exhortations. It crops out incidentally in many advocates of social changes. Thus Grönlund says : " A socialist régime will make it a man's *interest* to be honest; and just as surely as a stone falls to the ground, all men will become honest." Here seems to be an entire ignorance of what constitutes honesty as a virtue. Because a man does not steal from you or pick your pocket, he is not necessarily an honest man: you can simply predicate of him that he is not a pick-pocket, or that he is not a thief. The ox, satisfied with the rich pasturage of its grazing-field, feeds on, and does not jump the wall that divides it from the adjoining rocky pasture. That speaks well for its contented disposition, but it is not honesty. So it does not constitute a man of integrity to perform, as a cog-wheel in a machine, the work appointed him in some social régime. As a part of the machine, he has no idea what integrity means. According to the terms laid down, he has no more temptation to do differently than a stone has not to fall to the ground. The stone has just as much integrity, then, as the man: it is an honest stone, let me tell you that.

Here comes out plainly the radical defect of all such panaceas. They profess to furnish, once for all, the catholicon, or universal remedy for all the ills that social flesh is heir to.  All wants are to be supplied, all sufferings removed, all afflictions healed, by some external arrangements which money and modern improvements can furnish.  These will form a man's character, perfect his morals, purify his motives, and make him disinterested, manly, and loving!  That he shall form his own character is, of course, absurd.  Even Lamennais, whose deep spiritual sympathies were stirred, and whose interest was that of a man in the sufferings of his fellow-man, says that " from the holy maxims of equality, liberty and fraternity being immovably established, the organization of society will emanate."  But embody, if you will, these maxims in an external form, and how long will it last unless there is the internal spirit pervading its every part!  To gather brothers by blood under one roof has never yet proved a catholicon for an unbrotherly temper.

But in the system of Fourier all this demand for pure principles of action is regarded as sentimental bosh.  Society, he thinks, must be organized so as to give free expression to all the natural tendencies of man.  Self-restraint, self-control, and self-sacrifice are the fundamental errors of an effete and collapsing order of things.  The general harmony will come from the free action and re-action of all the affections, tendencies, and passions of man. So arrange the work, the occupations, and the amusements of life that every spontaneous passion shall find its proper gratification, and the great laws of social order will be established on the immutable basis of Nature's laws. When every part of the human machine, every wheel and pivot, is in its pre-arranged and proper place, there *must* be, he affirms, orderly movement and a harmonious result. There *can* be no such thing as suffering when every one can delight himself to the top of his bent, — an embodiment on the earth of Swedenborg's doctrine of the spiritual hells.

Such has been the rise and fall of some of the associations and phalanxes of the past; and in reading their history it is surprising, most of all, that while the ignorance, the moral defects, the social delinquencies, and the shortcomings of every kind are freely spoken of, the final failure is not attributed to these, but mainly to some external and material cause, — debt, poor crops, inharmonious surroundings, unfaithful agents, hasty preparation, barren soil, bad location, and insufficient capital. Thus, one of the members of the Sylvania association, of which Horace Greeley was treasurer, admits "that jealousies and ill-feelings were created, and in place of that self-sacrifice and zealous support of the constitution and officers, to which they were all pledged, there was a total disregard of all discipline, and a determination in each to have the biggest share of all things going, *except hard labor,* which was very unpopular with a certain class." But as if this were only a secondary matter, the writer goes on to say, " Aside from this, we had only a barren wilderness to experiment upon," etc.

And this association was announced as the remedy for "the present defective, vice-engendering, and ruinous system of society, with its wasteful complication of isolated households, its destructive competition and anarchy in industry, its constraint of millions to idleness," etc.

It is hard for us, at this day, remote from the stirring enthusiams of public meetings, the personal magnetism of leaders, the devoted zeal of long-pondering thought, and the hardships, perhaps, of a previous life of constraint and poverty, — it is hard for us to be patient with such utter want of commonsense, with the stupid futility of these numerous plans and attempts to cure, once for all, the diseases of modern society. One of these escaping victims well says, " If human beings were passive bodies, and we could place them just where we pleased, we might so arrange them that their actions would be harmonious." Yes; but this is a mighty *if,* that ought to be enough to deter any reflecting man from the attempt. And he goes on to say, " If we knew mathematically the laws which regulate the actions of human beings, it is possible we might place all men in true relations to one another."

Now, this is what Charles Fourier professed to have discovered and unfolded to humanity. As this very man says, " We wished to combine capital and labor, according to the theory laid down by Charles Fourier." It seems almost incredible that such men as Horace Greeley, Charles A. Dana, and others should have actively encouraged poor,

well-meaning enthusiasts to embark in such hazard-
ous schemes. They knew well enough, what these
earnest souls did not know, that Charles Fourier
discouraged all attempts to carry out his theory,
unless it could be carried out in its completeness
and under the circumstances indicated by him.
He laid down the exact forces of what he called
passional attraction, by which a harmonious adjustment would result, if a community were arranged
in such groups and series as some two thousand
persons might render possible, in a fitting phalanstery. And intelligent men who understood Fourier
sat by and saw these ignorant people embark in
an undertaking that was as sure to fail as the sun
was to set. It was as if some naval constructor
had said, "Build me a ship of such a size and of
such a strength, and you shall be insured safety in
crossing the stormiest ocean." And they build a
ship of reeds and shingles, and they call it *his*
modelled vessel, and put forth bravely to sea, and
sink, even before they have passed the harbor's
mouth! To float bogus mines and bonds of railroads that begin nowhere and end in the same
place, is harmless in comparison with this trifling
with man's most sacred aspirations and hopes.

Another association was started with a flourish-
ing constitution of sixty-two articles, of which the
fourteenth is as follows: —

"The treasury shall consist of a suitable metallic safe,
secured by seven different locks, the keys of which shall

be deposited in the keeping and the care of the following officers, to wit, — one with the president of the Unity, one with the president of the advisory council, one with the secretary-general, one with the agent-general, one with the arbiter-general, and one with the reporter-general. The moneys in said treasury to be drawn out only by authority of an order from the executive council, signed by all the members of the same in session at the time of the drawing of such order, and countersigned by the president of the Unity. All such moneys thus drawn shall be committed to the care and disposal of the executive council."

Here evidently was trust put not in human nature, but in a combination that beats the most elaborate modern combination-lock of the finest steel. No money, however, was lost; for none was ever put in, and the Unity itself soon became a zero.

To read the entire record of these attempts to overcome the great primal laws of Nature and humanity; to see often the best hearts broken under the fatal impingement against the rocky ramparts that the everlasting nature of things builds against ignorance, rashness, and vice, — leaves little room for ridicule or even blame. This world is but young, and the same lesson has to be learned again and again.

The day for forming such associations as a social catholicon has gone by, and the view of hopeful dreamers is fixed upon a far higher goal, — that is, of bringing all the power of the State to annihilate all individual property, all capital in private hands, and to effect all production and all distribution through public functionaries of the State.

But what is the State? Why, you and I. That is, then, you and I are to settle who of us shall occupy the land; who shall manage the railroads, the shops, and the manufactories; who shall create and distribute the vast and infinitely complex systems of modern life. According to Edward Bellamy, fifty years is an unreasonably long time for this universal revolution to be brought about. Incredible as it may seem, "Looking Backward" is a romance taken for more than gospel by thousands of men, and it has the greatest circulation of any book at the present time. This fact shows us not its literary worth, not its excellence as a work of pure imagination, but its adaptation to the thoughts and tendencies of the present time. A chord has been struck to which there is a general response. In this remarkable book the wishes and hopes and aspirings of many hearts are revealed; and though the special view it advocates may not be accomplished, the vision of better things than the present may be an incitement and an inspiration to many souls.

In the ancient view, man was really a man not from his own manliness, but as a corporate part of the city or State. So in the Augustinian view man was man as one of the elect of God, a citizen of the heavenly city. There was but one city that possessed this prerogative, — the earthly Rome; and it existed as the symbol of the city of God, into which the right of citizenship was the eternal decree of God himself. The Church received in a wider form the legacy of the city.

That any definite plan which man can devise, *à priori*, will be the final goal of humanity is a Utopian ideal. Man, as a recipient of the infinite reality, must ever be unfolding, putting forth higher aspirations, and using every present attainment as a stepping stone to yet more glorious ideals. The real heaven is in the enjoyment and use of this growing aspiration. It is not a discontented feeling arising from the want of some definite means of enjoyment, but of entire content with the means and conditions as adequate to man's real wants. To be absolutely perfect is, indeed, an impossible state for humanity; but to be content with an ever increasing growth of higher possibilities is the reward of fidelity to the opening ideals. In all ages, man has had the audacity to think that he can construct a model according to which society must be arranged, if it would reach a perfect state. It is forgotten that it would be easier to construct a living man than a living society. There is no limit to man's power in making machines; but social man is the most complex mechanism in Nature.

Because, moreover, man is this living, organized form of affections and spontaneous impulses; because he is subject to every skyey influence, and open to ever fresh inspirations of truth and duty, it is impossible to make him over after any one model, or distil any one simple or compound elixir that shall suit all his wants, or remedy all his social evils. As Mr. Ely says: "There is no one remedy for social evils. A multitude of agencies for good must work together." But does not he himself fall into this idea of a catholicon, panacea, or universal remedy, when he quotes with approval these words of De Laveleye: " There must be for human affairs an order which is the *best*. It is the order which ought to exist for the greatest happiness of the human race. It is for man to discover and establish it." Now, is the responsibility laid upon man to discover the *best* order for all the human race any more than to discover the best weather for the whole round earth? It is for man to adapt himself in the best way he can to those conditions of earth, sky, and atmosphere which prevail from hour to hour, in this climate and in that. He can establish, *à priori*, no one state of things which, being the absolutely best, will answer for all times and all men. There can be no one permanent, crystallized form that shall endure forever. To every human state there is a morning and an evening; for movement is the token and condition of life. While man lives, he must be in vital relations, ever changing, with that which surrounds him; and that which surrounds him reflects his own internal being. Any one fixed state would seem to a growing and unfolding soul an intolerable burden, a wearisome monotony of existence. Flat, stale, and unprofitable would become all the uses even of the best world into which we were nicely fitted to a T, parts of a machine from which there was no escape.

To the clear-seeing eye, society is *now* a form of useful activities, and not a mere conglomerate of scrambling, self-sufficing, all-grasping individualities. There is no honest work or business that is not founded upon the actual necessities of man, or which does not include the good of some others than self. Every paying employment, as well as many non-paying ones, ministers to some human need. To earn his own daily bread, the individual must perform some service to his fellow-men; and all the apparatus of social existence is for the supply of the varied wants of social man.

The more these wants are multiplied, the more easy it becomes to get what is called a living; and at the present time there are very many ways of ministering to the wants of society where fifty years ago there was one. The varieties of daily work are increasing from day to day; and it has been well said, that "every one who is lifted from a life of bare existence to one where it becomes a necessity for him to have the best of life, is adding so much to the world's wealth." In this way life becomes as great as we can make it.

A strenuous advocate of making all men public functionaries, says: "Look at the pettiness of isolated private business; and then consider what a dignity it will confer on one to become a public functionary, conscientiously contributing, in his smallest acts, to society's welfare!" But is not all the dignity really contained in that one mighty word "conscientiously"? Is not that included in the humblest work of every honest man and woman to-day?

Moreover, is it true that becoming a public functionary of itself adds to the dignity of a man's life? Does a man thereby become more manly, more self-sacrificing, broader in his views, grander in his outlook upon life and the world? Ask the post-office clerks, the members of the civil service, the men and women in Washington who serve in the official tread-mill, bitterly regretting the time when they stepped upon the revolving wheel, which now compels them to keep up, for dear life, the incessant tramp, tramp, tramp, of their convict round, — hear them speak of the pettiness of official life, and the illusion of any special dignity pertaining to the public functionary will be dispelled.

But whether as private individuals or as public functionaries, it matters not: the work of the all-aspiring soul that is present in Humanity, and is the central force of every unfolding adaptation to man's well-being and progress, — this work will be accomplished; and let us be glad that we are privileged to live and to learn in this day, when the dawn of a brighter morning gilds the distant mountain peaks.

# XII.

## SOCIAL TENDENCIES.

IN every organic structure there is a relation of all the parts to the whole; and when this relation is normal and perfect the object is beautiful, and answers all the purposes for which it was made. But when some one part, some one organ, is forced out of this relation, deformity is the result. Society may be deformed through undue predominance of king or lords or commons, when king, lords, and commons make up the whole. In different ages, different types of deformity are seen.

It has been well said that the three great characteristics of any living organism are unity, growth, and identity of structure. These characteristic features manifest themselves in that organism which we call the United States of America. The various parts are united as a vital whole; and of this whole, growth can most surely be predicated. So also can identity of structure. In England there is no such identity, for hereditary kingship and hereditary lords do not belong to a democratic structure.

In the social tendencies of to-day toward the carrying out of democratic principles into life, many see only danger to our present form of political organization. A recent writer in the "Atlantic Monthly" will have it that in the establishment of our government we were simply carrying out the principles and habits of constitutional history, but that now other influences have come in, to which we must adapt ourselves the best way we can; that, above all, leaders are necessary, and only in national leaders can national safety be found. He forgets the one great leader (*the people*) which makes leaders possible only as they share in the inspiration that comes to every soul; he does not consider that we shall hold together only so long as we are the conductors of the magnetic current that streams through all the race; that our safety and growth consist not in holding fast to any historical precedent, but in obeying the law of human progress, and in following that spirit of equal justice, of universal freedom, which was the key-note of the first intelligent political utterances.

But whether original or imported, we must accept the break which present tendencies — that order of things in which we live and work to-day — have made with the old. We hear it said: "True, *we* have a different way of governing, — we choose our rulers, and they do not theirs; that is about all you can make of it. It is a question, however, if their way may not be the best, — sometimes at least. To be sure, an hereditary ruler and a privileged class do not always produce the best results; and on the whole, if we can have a good strong police, it may not prove so bad a thing to have got rid of the expensive luxury of kings and queens, — especially if they have large families, and all the regal scions must have establishments and pensions, and be supported out of the public crib. Yet how nice it would be to have, as Mr. Carlyle says they have in England, ' a body of brave men and of beautiful, polite women, furnished *gratis*, as they are, — some of them (as my Lord Derby, I am told, in a few years will be) with not far from two-thirds of a million sterling annually!' Why could not we with profit have in America, as Mr. Carlyle suggests, ' a nobleman or two, with his chivalry and magnanimity, one polite in the finest form, — the politest kind of nobleman (especially his wife, the politest and gracefullest kind of woman)?'"

Now, greatly as we must admire bravery and magnanimity, devoutly as we may worship politeness and grace of demeanor, mere politeness and grace cannot make the sun go round the earth, even a little. Bravery and magnanimity must be developed in some more rational and consistent way than this. We must accept the break which our democratic order makes with the old order of things. "The breach of America," says the German Michelet,[1] "with the old principles is complete. America is to be called a *new* world, in the spiritual sense yet more than in the natural. Its connecting bond is the universal spirit. Its rulers are not the masters, but the servants of the people. It has no nobility, no privileged class with its ossi-

[1] History of the Development of Humanity since 1775.

fied prejudices, to hinder the transmission of the indwelling reason of the people, the divine inspiration. It has broken with historical precedents, and its *life is in the carrying out of the eternal new* which its Constitution embodies."

But we must distinguish between " breaking with historical precedents " and breaking with history itself. There is, there can be, no break in the life of humanity; and we are the normal development of the historic continuity of that humanity. That principle of life, that indwelling reason, that creating idea which gives meaning, continuity, and permanence to the political and social world, has in America found its ultimate and most universal expression. Take away this principle, and what meaning is there in all this material movement and multiform appearance of men and things? The new, different as it is, is the child of the old. It has a separate existence; but it has the blood of the parents coursing in its veins, though it must thereafter use its own lungs, and live by the beating of its own heart. Only thus can it build up a new body of a better type, and on a higher plane of social well-being.

The relation we have to the European world is sometimes spoken of as comprehended in showing the older nations that free institutions are possible, and that political arrangements after our pattern are the best method of governing a people. But this is a very incomplete and one-sided statement of this central truth, — that here, in America, is the unfolding and realization of principles and tendencies that are everywhere operating throughout the civilized world.  The form which such principles must take in *political* organization has here been taken.  In that direction the fitting expression has been found; the spirit has created its adapted body, and that work needs not to be done again.  And it is a universal law, that any spiritual tendency operates with full power only when it has reached the outmost boundary, the lowest plane of action and life; then it ascends, and pervades every part with fullest energy.  It became a vital necessity that slavery should be cut away; for it was a cancerous tumor in the body politic, sucking up the life and corrupting the blood.  It is a vital necessity that the fresh demands of the spirit of humanity to be embodied in other spheres of life than those of dynasties and diplomacies should meet a fitting response, and that ultimate forms be organized in which it can dwell.  The idea that each human being is to enjoy his full share in all that makes humanity great and beautiful and strong is here to grow brighter, even unto the perfect day.

Those questions which are imminent even now in European politics, — questions of forms of government, of proprietorship, of freedom of speech and the press, of privileges of birth and of class, of ancestral rights, of distribution of power, of civil and ecclesiastical jurisdiction, — are settled here; and they interest us only as being the initial movements of that tendency everywhere at work.  Certain external institutions are not in harmony with the democratic spirit in the British empire; and if the democratic spirit is to have sway, those institutions must go, in spite of conservative fears and reluctant tenacity of possession. " It is impossible," says one, " to reconcile hereditary privilege with civil equality of rights; and while this antagonism exists, under forms however venerated, there will always accompany it a sense of instability and feeling of uncertainty with regard to national action, and a never ending source of national conflict." [1]

In America we have done with discussing the rights of Church and State, of king and subject; we have not to contend for theoretical freedom, or to overthrow hierarchies, orders, and hereditary establishments. We begin where this, as an ideal, ended. Our theory assumes the essential manhood of every man, and regards institutions as but the means of perfecting *that*. We believe that every man is in all essential rights equal to every other man; that every man is a priest and a king; that no pope can add to his royalty by any consecrating oil, no ruler can confer upon him any civil right, no outward dignity can exact his homage. As man, he enters upon an inheritance of infinite freedom and unbounded progress. The law which he obeys, he obeys because it has first been enacted in his own soul; its validity is not in any outside ordinance, but in the tribunal of his own heart. He

---

[1] The Political Life of our Time. By D. Nicol.

is governor as well as governed, law-maker as well
as citizen, judge as well as executive.   Here is scope
for the individual and social application of every
truth in education, morals, and political science, —
for the application of every ideal that human aspiration has ever framed, every grace, every magnanimity, every service that the lover of God or man
has nurtured in rarest moments of insight, or in
his most enthusiastic dreams.   The currents of humanly inspiring life flow all within and around; and
so far as a man is open to their influence, he rises
into elements of fresh strength and use.

The central principle, then, which pervades our
national organic structure is manhood.    Its *political* expression is a common-place of oratorical
appeal; but its operation as a beneficent, conser-
vating principle of social order and development is
not yet fully acknowledged, or even clearly perceived.   We ought to see that it is not destructive,
but constructive; not to be feared, but welcomed;
not disorganizing and disintegrating, but healing
and organific in all its normal applications.

The difficulty in effecting this normal adjustment
of life to the political theory is enhanced by the
operation of influences that come from the mighty
revolution taking place in the industrial sphere.
Thousands are made rich and other thousands are
made poor by the changes that take place in the
business world.   A millionnaire is made by some
unexpected rise in the value of land, some discovery
of oil or coal or iron or copper, by some rise in

merchandise or in stocks; a city suddenly springs up, and a farmer's potato field is of more value than a gold mine; a fashion changes, and some prosperous manufacture is destroyed, and an entire community sees its daily bread suddenly imperilled; a selfish greed of some railroad or bank officers wrecks the institutions intrusted to them, and helpless poverty stares thousands in the face. By the division and sub-division of labor, and the dominating power of capital, it gets to be harder and harder for the workman to become a capitalist, or even to save a few dollars from his daily wages. The temptations to extravagance, to display, to luxurious indulgence are multiplied on every side, and there is much that looks like a justification in fact of Carlyle's expression, so dubious in point of taste, — "the universal rush into the cheap and nasty in manners and life."

Is it any wonder that Young America sometimes gets heated up beyond the boiling point, and boils over, with much foaming and sizzling and waste? Reverence does seem to be at an awful discount; and modest, patient merit, sitting on the back seats, appears to get but a small share of confectionery and ice-cream. But whatever form of disorder and discomfort, even direful suffering, may result, it is only a temporary and transitional concomitant, and will disappear with the rise in the general level of thought, and the higher tone imparted by universal education, — in a word, by the prevalence of the principle itself in its full working power. The grand army, with its disciplined ranks and orderly march, comes to protect and upbuild; while the petty marauding and pilfering of hen-roosts and pig-pens are by the skirmishers and flying scuds, the " bummers" of the host.  In giving all a chance for wealth, we must not be surprised if some rich miner's spouse keeps her carriage, and smokes her clay pipe as her thoroughbreds sweep her along in all the majesty of a coach-and-six; if some suddenly created millionnaire adorns with a necklace of gold nuggets or diamonds his favorite hound, or takes su-preme delight in seeing wife or daughter sparkling all over with flashing gems like a phosphorescent wave; if some substantial citizen gains an *entrée* to some foreign court, and, his early years having been under some other master than a master of ceremo-nies, he says even to the Pope, " Well, old fellow, how's your wife and family?  Hope they are well; " or to some royal exile, as one of our well-meaning citizens said to the exiled Louis Napoleon, who spoke of having visited our country twenty years before, " I hope, sir, we may have the pleasure of welcoming you there again."  But what matters it that there are some exuberances of taste, and a boiling-over of individual idiosyncracies of vulgar-ity and conventional disrespect?  They are only the natural results of a want of culture that was the normal state of the past.

At any rate, there has been in America no lavish bestowment of the wealth, the lands, the honors, and the educational means of a people in order to give an exaggerated cultivation and refinement to a privileged few. Grant even that there be now a lack of original and genetic power in the highest departments of knowledge and art, yet the average level is continually becoming higher, and a better tone pervades the common life, from generation to generation. And the highest will come whenever the superstructure beneath shall be fitted for it; the dome shall crown fittingly the vast cathedral of humanity, — a dome which only such walls could bear, not those propped and suspended by artificial means. We want no elevation produced by compression at the sides, but an elevation that comes from the building up of the whole mass with solid masonry and architectural skill. The thought, the manners, the education, the literature of our civilization must be based on the manhood of the whole people, on the popular life, — working from foundation to topstone, from seed to tree, from tree to forest. We do not look for a few isolated and gigantic monarchs of the plain, the survivors of companions long since rotted away, perishing in their feeble and stunted growth, but for plantations of noble trees over vast areas of field and hill-side, prairie and mountain-range, from the Atlantic to the Pacific shore.

Were they not so saddening, the wailings over this state of things from that once glorious prophet of universal brotherhood, Carlyle, would be highly ludicrous. He sees only " the going of democracy to complete itself in the bottomless, . . . a free ra-

cing, not in shop-goods only, but in all things temporal, spiritual, and eternal, — a beautiful career to
be flung generously open, wide as the portals of the
universe; so that everybody shall start free, — and
everywhere, under enlightened popular suffrage, the
race shall be to the swift, and the high office shall
fall to him who is ablest, if not to do it, at least
to get elected for doing it." But is this, in the
main, so bad? Is not this free and open career,
this equal chance for all, what the ages have been
striving after? That the way to knowledge, the way
to wealth, and the way to honorable position should
be not a narrow foot-path to be trod by wayfarers
in single file, but a broad avenue wherein every
man can walk without jostling his fellow, — is this
to be sneered at and ridiculed? In "Sartor Resar-
tus" there is the following passage, worthy of being
inscribed in letters of gold : —

"Venerable to me is the hard hand, crooked, coarse;
wherein, notwithstanding, lies a cunning virtue, indefea-
sibly royal, as of the sceptre of this planet. Venerable,
too, is the rugged face, all weather-tanned, besoiled, with
its rude intelligence; for it is the face of a man living
manlike. Oh, but the more venerable for thy rudeness,
and even because we must pity as well as love thee!
Hardly-treated brother! for us was thy back so bent,
for us were thy straight limbs and fingers so deformed;
thou wert our conscript, on whom the lot fell, and fighting our battles thou wert so marred. For in thee, too,
lay a God-created form, but it was not to be unfolded;
encrusted must it stand, with the thick adhesions and de-

facements of labor; and thy body, like thy soul, was not to know freedom. Alas! while the body stands so broad and brawny, must the soul lie blinded, dwarfed, stupefied, almost annihilated? That there should one man die ignorant who had capacity for knowledge, this I call a tragedy, were it to happen more than twenty times a minute, as by some computations it does. The miserable fraction of science, which united mankind has acquired, — why is not this, with all diligence, imparted to all?"

A very reasonable question this, which our forefathers long ago asked themselves, and which they and we have been doing our best to make the asking hereafter unnecessary.

But our prophet goes on in these words: —

"Quite in an opposite strain is the following: 'The old Spartans had a wiser method; they went out and hunted down their Helots, and speared and spitted them when they grew too numerous. With our improved fashions of hunting, now after the invention of firearms and standing armies, how much easier were such a hunt! Perhaps in the most thickly peopled country some three days annually might suffice to shoot all the able-bodied paupers that had accumulated within the year. Let governments think of this."

An opposite strain, with a vengeance! But it was the strain which he continued for thirty years. It was because he had no faith in an inspired humanity; because he looked not to the many, but to the few, — not to the instinctive powers within man, but to a force outside of him, — that he therefore invoked the Alarics, the scourges of God, the besoms of destruction. Or if there is to be salvation from chaos, he thinks the nobility must practise rhythmic drills with their peasantry and dependents! (Always higher and lower, never equality.) He wants the "good old English gentleman" to appear again on the scene, and servants' and laborers' wages, at so many shillings a day, to be utterly abolished. He recommends some "combined rhythmic action" to be introduced among laborers; but mark the condition, for it indicates a great deal, — " always," he says, "always to be instituted by *some superiors from above.*" And he goes on to say: "I believe that the vulgarest cockney crowd, flung out millionfold on a Whit-Sunday, with nothing but beer and dull folly to depend on for amusement, would at once kindle into something human if you set them to do almost any regulated act in common, and would dismiss their beer and dull foolery in the silent charm of rhythmic human companionship, in the practical feeling, *probably new,* that all of us are made, in an unfathomable way, brothers to one another."

Now, how can men be made to feel that they are brothers, unless they are treated in a brotherly way? The "practical feeling" will come, when the fact is realized, — never before. The people are not fools; they are not to be impressed very deeply with the fact of brotherhood through rhythmic drills and gingerbread, and smiles dispensed by "superiors from above." When the institutions and the class feelings they cherish are dissolved, whether in the weltering chaos of Niagara or in the warm atmosphere of a common humanity, there will be no need of special drills from noblemen, of special sugar-plums from high-born ladies, or of special grape-shot from kings.

But a notable phenomenon presents itself. These superiors, who are alone to be intrusted with the direction of the rhythmic movement of this dull, vulgar set of artisans and laborers, — these highly refined men and gracious ladies have no " rhythmic combination " to impart. Their condition, after all, is not an enviable one even in the eyes of their too devout worshipper; for Mr. Carlyle goes on to describe in pathetic terms their melancholy status: " More than once," he says, " I have been affected with a deep sorrow and respect for noble souls among our aristocracy, for their high stoicism, and silent resignation to a kind of life which they individually could not alter, and saw to be so empty and paltry." Has it then come to this, that men on whom fortune has lavished her choicest favors, — houses in town and houses in the country, horses and parks, conservatories and yachts, galleries of art and libraries, gardens and bank-accounts; men to whose education all the ages have been made tributary, and in whose behalf the millions have been stunted and subsidized, — that these men are to be respected simply for their stoicism, their noble endurance under all these harrowing burdens, and their stern resignation to leading " empty and paltry " lives? Yes, it has come to this; and it

must come to this.   Not even an English nobleman
can dodge the law of gravitation; not even he can
escape the operation of the social, human Nemesis.
" If one member suffer, all the members suffer
with it; " and if all the members are suffering, how
shall the one escape?   According to Carlyle, to
accept the new civilization is to " shoot Niagara."
Well, better that, if *that* is the only way of righting things, with the assurance that what may come
after that plunge is just as much under the impartial
laws of a universe that shines and rains on the just
and the unjust, as anything that came before.   But
obedience to these laws will make life so grand and
joyous that all the artificial and exclusive forms of
aristocratic pretence shall indeed seem " empty and
paltry," a dim shadow cast by the light which they
absorbed but could not reflect.

The present condition of English society is
treated by a prominent Review under the head of
" Social Disintegration."   This consists, it is said,
in a want of personal acquaintance and intercourse
between the higher and lower classes.   Of these extremes in the body politic the writer predicates " a
mutual ignorance, and an incapacity to understand
each other, that may almost be called dangerous."
Higher and lower classes! — he does not see that
they already understand each other too well.   They
understand each other sufficiently well to know that
by no possibility can the gulf between them be filled
up with kindly inquiries after one's health and the
sick baby; with occasional dinners for the peas-

antry and mugs of foaming beer. The patriarchal age — all the giving on the one side, and all the receiving as a lordly boon on the other — is fast vanishing away. The old, severed, personal ties must be replaced by others as real, and as adapted to present wants and conditions, as were those of old to the times in which they had their rise. "The moral unity" of the people must be established on a different basis; and when once established, it can never be secure, until the laws of spiritual gravitation have produced that equilibrium which comes from the centre of gravity resting upon the lowest point of support.

What is stable equilibrium in natural philosophy? Is it not, that, when disturbed from its state of rest, a body tends of itself to return to that state; and that this will always be the case when the centre of gravity is lowest in its position? And here is the precise point of difference between the old and the new social order. In the old, that point of stable equilibrium does not exist, as the different classes of society form entirely separate organizations, with views and interests that are utterly irreconcilable; while in the new, whatever changes take place are only the development and application, to the various details of life, of what constitutes now the animating principle of national existence. But the vastest iceberg floating in unstable equilibrium in the Atlantic sea must oscillate and roll over until the eternal law shall vindicate itself, and that force which sun and mote obey shall accomplish its work.

A further indication of the new order, and a derivation from the central principle of manhood, is the idea of educated labor, — the reconciliation of brain and hand, of thought and work,  Not he is to be envied who can point to his ancestor's kingship in the social realm, but he who has found his work and takes delight in doing it.  The vast needs and opportunities, the open career for every talent and faculty, invite to work for some noble and useful end.  To be a worker in aught that ministers to human benefit is the best foundation for wealth and position in the world.  From no work-bench or trade or employment is the pathway closed to him who follows the clew which industry, skill, and science put into his hand.  In the very place where each man stands, there where his foot is planted, he can make all the past tributary to his growth; and from the sure basis of Nature and practical life he can become the thinker, the inventor, the captain of labor, the master-workman, the founder of some beneficent industry, some wide-spreading means of good.  Foolish notions of the past still trouble some foolish heads; and manly work is ignorantly and — as they come afterward to see — stupidly dodged.  But the fact is patent that the leaders spring up from the ranks of toil, from a youth nurtured in hardship, from the healthy lap of Nature, from those early thrown upon themselves.

Occasionally, even in this country, a survival of the old civilization crops out in the words " lower classes," " the common mass," " vulgar herd," " ser-

vile occupation," "mere mechanic," etc.; for our
system retains some of the virus of the old Greek
and Roman times, and of times not so very remote
in a large part of the United States, when to get
one's honest living by labor was to be a slave;
when no one performed manual labor but slaves, or
the sons of slaves. But the all-pervading spirit of
our modern civilization renders it more and more
impossible to separate learning and labor, art and
every-day practical life. The new civilization is not
the separation of thought and work, but their reconciliation and atonement; it is not a pampered man
of letters on the one hand and a sordid drudge on
the other, but a harmonious development of brain
and hand, of body and mind. So far as this tendency becomes realized, life gains in breadth, — in
extent of services rendered and services received; in
fulness of aspiration, and in earnest devotedness.

Says an inquirer into socialism: [1] —

"The democratic movement is just beginning, and it is
rather early to pass sentence upon it; but of this at least
we may be sure, — that the people who think that the democracy consists [alone] of vote by ballot, and that everything else will proceed in the old style, will be grievously
disappointed."

No, it will not proceed in the old style; neither
will it proceed in the style of the anarchists of to-
day, or in that of the early French Revolutionists,

[1] An Inquiry into Socialism. By Thos. Kirkup. Page xxiii.
London, 1887.

intoxicated as they were with the first vintage of
freedom and equality.   That fire has not indeed
burned itself out, but it has burned up the brush-
wood and the combustible materials on the surface.
Yet the central fire remains; and in its heat the
huge structures of evil will be dissolved, and higher
forms of social life will be the heritage of the
coming generations.

The forces now at work are not to be judged
of by the outbursts of a few enthusiasts enamored
with their own plans, with their own short-sighted
view of human history and human development.
They must, indeed, speak their word; but deeper
voices, like the sound of many waters, are uttering
words of better cheer.

What are some of these encouraging aspects?

First, there is the tendency to give free and unrestricted action to natural and social laws; and these
carry with them their own redeeming power.   As
the domain of Nature passes over to man, what were
once exclusive benefits become diffused among the
many as a common possession; the universal heritage enlarges for every man.   As obstructions are
removed, the new organizes itself, and needs no interference of theoretic systems or rhythmic plans.
The organization itself is beyond human insight
or human skill, but it is gradually being developed.
The tendencies of our modern civilization necessarily increase, at every step, the mutual depen-
dence of man upon his fellow-men.   Society is
becoming a network in which the minutest thread

cannot be spared, and the least stitch is essential to the perfectness of the woven whole. If you are a manufacturer, a railroad director, an employer of any kind, the law will more and more hold you responsible for every neglect of the health and life of him whom you employ.

Secondly, the legislation of every country that has a representation of the people is directed toward great questions of social interests and measures of popular benefit. Thus, as the latest example, the cable telegraph informs us that "Lord Randolph Churchill, in a public letter, urges the Conservatives, during the coming session of the British Parliament, to give prominence to the land-law measures for the reform of workingmen's dwellings, laborer's allotments and licensing, and laws providing for shorter hours of labor, etc." Yes, this is to be the work of conservatives themselves, and is not to be left to the radicals : Balaam, though in the pay of the other side, must bless and not curse. So too, in our country, the people themselves, as an organic body, are gradually seeking to reform abuses, to prevent injustice, and to give to every child the means of education, in order that he may find that career in which he may be most useful to his fellowmen. As a sign of the times, let us hear what an eminent citizen said in a letter not long ago, declining to be a candidate for mayor : —

"The public schools are not abreast with the times, and will not be until manual training, judiciously added to our present system, sends out all boys and girls, rich and poor, trained in eyes and fingers as well as brain, for success in life. . . .

" The pauper and neglected children should be placed on a farm, where in cottages containing not over thirty inmates, and under the charge of superintendents who could teach different branches of industry, they might grow up with the least possible institution taint. . . .

" The street commissioners need strong impulse in favor of modest streets for the homes of plain people in suitable locations. . . .

" The welfare of the working-classes needs to be considered with devoted attention. . . .

" The hours of labor can be shortened, especially where skill, education, or the use of machinery aids the workingman. . . .

" Many small play-grounds for children should be provided throughout the city."

Now, all this is in the direction which a true civilization points out, and whether particular measures are expedient or not remains to be determined by those whom the people elect to do their bidding. But a force, which no conservative view of the limitations of municipal power can turn aside, tends in the direction of doing what may be done for the common benefit.

But, lastly, the modern social tendencies are the direct outgrowth of the spirit of Christianity itself. Fifty years ago I said in an oration on the oneness of Christianity and Democracy : " The humble flower has found many to interpret its silent language; the stars have had their prophetic seers to unfold their mysteries; and now the common of every-day life, the despised of every-day labor, have found their priests, and in Christianity their secret is revealed. A true democracy and a true Christianity are one."

# XIII.

## THE NATION AS AN ORGANISM IN SHAKSPEARE.

MR. MULFORD says that the very "condition of political science is the apprehension of the truth that the nation is an organism." It is indeed a vital necessity in the present phase of economic thought; and it may not be out of place to show how something of this organic life reveals itself in Shakspeare's universal drama. Not that Shakspeare consciously proposed to himself any such thesis, or had in view any such social ends as may be made out to be the drift of some of his characters and representations. But every truly great artist in accomplishing one end accomplishes many others. He presents universal truths, and expresses without being aware of it those vital relations which could not by any possibility have been within the range of conscious vision. Thus Shakspeare is the unfolder of the organic life of the nation or State, and his personages cannot live and act without revealing something of common membership and of national unity.

This great dramatist looks upon the State as an organic body, — a social form deriving its powers, its duties, its very life-blood from the one spirit

pervading all its members. Of society as originating
in an agreement between individuals, or constituted
by isolated atoms, he knows and says nought.
" Great is the mystery of the soul of State " is the
thought that inspires every reference to men as
corporate beings, — to rulers and ruled; to kings
and subjects; to princes and beggars. There is
an internal, vital connection between all parts of
the body politic, not merely an external association; from this vital union no humblest part can
be severed without causing suffering and anguish
throughout. As in the human body, so in the body
politic there is a gradation of honor and dignity de-
pending upon the closeness of relationship to the
common-weal and the service rendered to the entire body. The disturbance of this equilibrium of
powers and destinies must therefore always be at-
tended with wide-spread disaster.

> " The cease of majesty
> " Dies not alone, but like a gulf doth draw
> What 's near it with it. It is a massy wheel
> Fixed on the summit of the highest mount,
> To whose huge spokes ten thousand lesser things
> Are mortised and adjoined ; which, when it fall,
> Each small annexment, petty consequence,
> Attends the boisterous ruin. Never alone
> Did the king sigh, but with a general groan." [1]

This truth is stated in a more positive form in
" Troilus and Cressida." The wise Ulysses, declaring
the reason why Troy still stands, says, —

[1] Hamlet, act iii. scene 3.

> " Oh, when degree is shaked,
> Which is the ladder to all high designs,
> Then enterprise is sick ! "

So the key-note of history is struck in " Richard II.," where the summary is made of what the succeeding plays detail with such dramatic force: —

> " Oh, if you raise this house against this house,
> It will the woefullest division prove
> That ever fell upon this cursed earth !
> Prevent it, resist it, let it not be so,
> Lest child, child's children, cry against you ' woe ! ' "

No Greek drama, with its ancestral fate, has ever portrayed in deeper colors the law of social retribution immanent in the life of succeeding generations.

The difference between that government which is a social organism, a living unity, and that which is a mechanical contrivance made up of pieces that can be dealt with separately, is plainly seen in Shakspeare. He treats the State as a commonweal, a living body, no part of which can be punctured or disturbed without disturbing all the others. Every part, to insure health, must work in harmony with every other part. Each organ, tissue, muscle, and nerve must obey the common impulse to maintain circulation and reach the end of complete life. No organ has an independent agency. As a statesman says in " Henry V.," —

> " For government, though high and low and lower,
> Put into parts, doth keep in one consent ;
> Congreeing in a full and natural close,
> Like music."

Still further to unfold the vital nature of the social organism, its essential oneness, under the "divers functions," is illustrated from the honey-bees, —

> " Creatures, that, by a rule in Nature, teach
> The act of order to a peoplèd kingdom."

In a monarchy the king is the head, and no one can harm him without bringing " the whole kingdom into desolation," as Henry says. But the sympathy between the different members of the same body, however named, is the point to be considered. There is nothing in the mere name of king. Shakspeare is not dazzled by the glitter of royal station; manhood is as essential to the king as to any citizen. His pre-eminent place, indeed, calls for preeminent strength and attractive power. The mere outside is nothing; the title brings with it a compensating trouble. As Brakenbury moralizes on the situation of the Duke Clarence, —

> " Princes have but their titles for their glories,
> An outward honor for an inward toil;
> And, for unfelt imagination,
> They often feel a world of restless cares."[1]

This deposition of the king as a fetich, and this proclamation of a common humanity appear from two quarters as opposite as the poles, and yet each utterance converging to the same point, — King Richard II. and King Henry V. The former, — faithless to every kingly duty, yet fondly trusting that the very stones of his native kingdom will

---

[1] Richard III., act i. scene 4.

have a feeling in his behalf, and rise up, armed soldiers, to fight for him, although he himself has alienated every soldierly heart, — asks how they can call him king, in " whose crown death keeps his court," who suffers hunger and thirst like other men, and who " feels want and tastes grief." Inasmuch as he is subject to these human limitations, he asks: " How can you say to me I am a king ? " How, indeed ? And so he gives " the pride of kingly sway from out his heart," and washes away with his tears all oaths of allegiance and fealty, —

> " With mine own tongue deny my sacred state,
> With mine own breath release all duty's rites."

Still further to unfold the lesson that a kingdom is a kingdom only when " law, form, and due proportion " are kept, there is that striking scene between the gardener and his servants, where he says to them, —

> " Cut off the heads of too fast growing sprays,
> That look too lofty in *our* commonwealth :
> All must be *even* in *our* government."

And afterward this wise gardener says, —

> " Bolingbroke
> Hath seized the wasteful king.  Oh what pity is it,
> That *he* had not so trimmed and dressed *his* land
> As we this garden ! "

Here is a memorable lesson out of the book of royal duties, to be taught by a player from his pulpit-stage. But the like regal ethics come from the mouth of one who.in " every inch" showed himself a king, — the chivalrous, manly, heroic Henry V. Shakspeare shows his deep insight into the difference between man in his nakedness and man in his social apparel in that soliloquy of Henry before the battle of Agincourt, when, moralizing upon his condition and that of the common soldier, he says, —

> " O ceremony, show me but thy worth!
> Art thou aught else but place, degree, and form,
> Creating awe and fear in other men? "

Because the king is so differentiated from other men, he must watch, must lead, must truly be a king. Yes, Shakspeare saw clearly this truth, which Carlyle illustrated in such a variety of ways, — " that, first, man is a spirit, and bound by invisible bonds to all men; secondly, that he wears clothes, which are the visible emblems of that fact."

But clothes are only rags, unless they clothe something. Whatever commands, must have the right which comes from fitness and power. He who assumes a divine commission must be divinely commissioned, — or, woe upon his head! He only can lead whom Nature sanctions by giving him insight, self-control, the magic of personal authority, the secret word at whose utterance doors fly open, and the genii of Nature throng to do service. King Richard II. looks into the glass, and finding no kingly image reflected, dashes it to pieces. Henry

V., is ready to die, alone, honorably with the king. Every nerve within him thrills with the feeling that he is a king.

The queen's son, poor Cloten, in "Cymbeline," finds this out when he comes in contact with one in whom, as Belarius says, divine Nature, the goddess, "blazons herself." The clothes-horse and the man thus reveal themselves : —

> *Cloten.*                    Yield thee, thief !
> *Guiderius.* To who ? — to thee ? What art thou ? Have not I
> An arm as big as thine ? a heart as big ?
> Thy words, I grant, are bigger ; for I wear not
> My dagger in my mouth.   Say what thou art ;
> Why should I yield to thee ?
> *Cloten.* Thou villain base, knowest me not by my clothes ?
> *Guiderius.* No, nor thy tailor, rascal,
> Who is thy grandfather : he made those clothes,
> Which, as it seems, make thee."

They proceed to fight, and he in whom the divine goddess Nature "blazons herself," cuts off the head of the clothes-dummy and throws it into the creek, with the contemptuous words, —

> "Let it to the sea,
> And tell the fishes he 's the queen's son, Cloten.
> That 's all I reck."

And when told that on account of his dead foe being a prince, reverence for his high place should lead to a princely burial, this peerless son of Nature accedes, but says in his off-hand way, out of " an invisible instinct," —

" Pray you, fetch him hither.
Thersites' body is as good as Ajax',
When neither are alive."

But Shakspeare goes further than the verbal statement that mankind reduced to a state of pure nature find one common level: he puts kings and dukes themselves upon the stage stripped of all their dignities and ceremonies, and glad to find refuge in the meanest hut and on the dirtiest straw. King Lear, the representative of purely arbitrary sovereignty, shaking off all cares and business on younger strength, expects still to keep all the ceremonies, — " still retain the name and all the additions to a king."

It cannot be. In unclothing himself of the kingdom he divested himself of all power, and became involuntarily a subject to that "Nature" to whose law Edmund voluntarily bound himself as his goddess. The latter rebels against " that plague of custom," that " curiosity of nations," or, in other words, that strict rule of civil institutions which made him, as an illegitimate son, no lawful heir of his father's dukedom. " Fine word, — *legitimate !* " he exclaims; he will trust to his own wit, and if his " invention thrive," and " the gods stand up for bastards," he will prosper to his heart's content. No ceremony shall stand in the path of his advancement. He fights it out on this line, with a courage and an inventive grasp worthy of a better cause. He fails; for what is the wit of one man against the omnipotent laws of social order? What is the

keenest intellect against the on-striding Nemesis of
outraged moral ordinance?  He who holds in possession half the kingdom, of which Lear had dispos-
sessed himself, falls by the hand of a peasant-slave,
who rises in his manhood to plead against cruelty,
and hinder his prince from tearing out the eye of
the helpless Duke Gloster.  " A *peasant* stand up
thus? " exclaims the Duke Cornwall in disgust and
anger, as he runs at him with his sword; but he is
himself slain, for he " takes the chance of anger,"
and throwing away all the advantage which ceremony gave him, — stripped naked of that, — he
goes to the wall as the inferior man.  Upon the
three daughters of the king poison, steel, and the
hangman's ropes how all their *natural* as well as
social virtues, and they perish by deaths as miserable as ever beset the meanest of villains and the
lowest of slaves.

Now, what have we here?  A quarry of dead game
to please the bloodthirsty taste of that bloodthirsty
age?  A holocaust of victims to satiate the degraded
craving of that London populace which saw men's
ears and noses slit, their heads cut off, their bodies
burned and exposed to tortures that cannot now be
described without making the flesh creep, — which
saw all this not on the mimic stage alone, but in real,
every-day life?  No; here we have one common
theme, — man freed from social bonds; man reduced to and falling back upon his natural, savage
instincts; man with none of the defences that organized society — with laws, well ordered government,

humane institutions — throws around men as barriers against the encroachments of passionate will
and arbitrary injustice. The whole play, with its
characters interesting us in every change of passion,
every least utterance, every flush of countenance,
every accent of grief or joy, hope or despair, — the
whole is a picture of social misery, and of the barbarism of humanity when dissolved into its primeval
elements; though the actors were dukes and dukes'
bravest sons, kings and kings' fairest daughters.

Thrown back into the old Celtic times, who
could suspect that the mirror was held up to the
poet's own age, or that he was unveiling the depths
of disorganized social life? Yet it is a thin disguise
which is continually dropped. Think of an apothe-
cary giving "an ounce of civet" to sweeten a poor
king's imagination! think of Lear's extemporized
court of justice, where "yond justice rails upon
yond simple thief," and when they "change places,
handy-dandy, which is the justice, which is the
thief?" where the rascal beadle is bidden to hold
his bloody hand, — bloody with lashing a poor
strumpet, — and the usurer hangs the cozener;
where one is told to get for himself "glass eyes,
and like a scurvy politician *seem* to see the things"
he does not really see! — think of all this, and the
old Celtic film and background disappear, and the
poet's time sits for its picture. Shakspeare was
not mindful of what the critics call local coloring:
verily he was not, — for the great, present humanity
pressed him in on every side!

In this play the entire order of things is sub-
verted. The social state is turned topsy-turvy; the
king is forced from the wild natural elements to
seek the shelter of a hovel, after fleeing from his
own child's inhospitable roof into the waste and
storm-pelted heath; the would-be friend, giving
way to impatient anger, becomes the worst of foes;
the loyal, virtuous son of wealth and station assumes
the vilest garb and name, and can only save his life
by abjuring home and name and reason itself;
and in telling what he will do, he but describes
what was a common sight in Shakspeare's own
time, the glorious Elizabethan age: —

> "My face I 'll grime with filth;
> Blanket my loins; elf all my hair in knots;
> And with presented nakedness out-face
> The winds and persecutions of the sky.
> The country gives me proof and precedent
> Of bedlam beggars, who with roaring voices
> Strike in their numbed and mortified bare arms
> Pins, wooden pricks, nails, sprigs of rosemary;
> And with this horrible object, from low farms,
> Poor pelting villages, sheep-cotes and mills,
> Sometime with lunatic bans, sometime with prayers,
> Enforce their charity."

So low is this scion of a dukedom reduced, that he
welcomes even the assumption of a false name, —
"Poor Tom is something, Edgar is nothing,"

In this universal subversion, the fool is the only
wise man, and the madman the only sane head, —
the pivot upon which the final success depends.

The fool knows why a man's nose stands in the middle of his face; why a snail has a house; why the seven stars are no more than seven; and what a man will learn by going to school to the ant. And, withal, the fool is loyal as well as wise: he serves for love and not for gain. He sings, —

> "That sir which serves and seeks for gain,
>     And follows but for form,
> Will pack when it begins to rain,
>     And leave thee in the storm.
> But I will tarry; the fool will stay,
>     And let the wise man fly:
> The knave turns fool that runs away;
>     The fool no knave, perdy.

No knave, and no fool either; for he sees in his glimmering way a moral, or universal lesson, in this particular case, and he draws that moral: —

> "The man that makes his toe
>     What he his heart should make
> Shall of a corn cry woe,
>     And turn his sleep to wake."

A fool's doggerel, indeed, but pregnant with all the wisdom of modern social ethics. From the earliest times, society has made a toe of what should have been the heart; and it has cried out, and is at intervals crying out, because of the tender corn which is afflicting it with spasm, and which disturbs its sleep. "You are the great toe of this assembly," said the aristocratic Menenius to the loudest of the popular rabble; but that great toe, the real heart of Rome, trodden upon and trodden upon for ages, became at last gangrened, and the whole body succumbed to death.

Shakspeare has given us in his world-wide representation two social insurrections, — that of Rome in the third century of the city,[1] and that headed by Jack Cade in the fifteenth century of our era.[2] They are both put down, not by a righting of the wrongs and miseries of the rabble, but by the pressure of a foreign war, and by that appeal to patriotism against a foreign nation which has always quelled the fiercest domestic troubles. The old barrel, ready to fall to pieces, is hooped together by this device of uniting against an external enemy. Jack Cade's final exclamation, when the fickle rabblement shout for the king and Clifford, who is to lead them against France, is, —

"Was ever feather so lightly blown to and fro as this multitude? The name of Henry the Fifth hales them to an hundred mischiefs, and makes them leave me desolate. . . . In despite of the devils and hell, have through the very midst of you ! And Heavens and honor be witness, that no want of resolution in me, but only my followers' base and ignominious treasons, makes me betake me to my heels."

In Coriolanus, the cry of the suffering plebs is well voiced. When appealed to as "*good* citizens,"

---

[1] Coriolanus, act i. scene i.
[2] Henry VI. Part ii. act iv. scene 8.

one of them says: " *We* are accounted poor citizens; the patricians, good. What authority surfeits on would relieve us. If they would yield us but the superfluity, while it were wholesome, we might guess they relieved us humanely; but they think we are too dear. The leanness that afflicts us, the object of our misery, is as an inventory to particularize their abundance; our sufferance is a gain to them." And when told that the patricians "have most *charitable care*" of the people, the same citizen replies: " Care for us! True, indeed! They ne'er cared for us yet. Suffer us to famish, and their storehouses crammed with grain; make edicts for usury, to support usurers; repeal daily any wholesome act established against the rich, and provide more piercing statutes daily to chain up and restrain the poor! If the wars eat us not up, *they* will; and *there's* all the love they bear *us!* " It can pass on the stage as a representation of what happened two thousand years ago in Rome, and pass without question as to whether "there is any offence in the argument." But that cry is still heard, and will be heard until there is some answer given that shall be something more than a sop for the temporary passion and the momentary greed.

Thus is to be seen in Shakspeare the clearly expressed idea that the men called a nation, a people, a State, constitute one organized form, in which each part has life only as it shares in the

life of the whole; and the life of the whole inter-
penetrates and sustains each individual organ or
part. The king, separate and isolated, has no
power or even existence in himself; the lowest and
meanest part, while organically related, has a meaning in Nature, has a right to be, and shares in the
universal life. The most potent individuality cut
off from this life is lost as a moral force. Coriolanus, the hero, — the towering, proud, self-sufficient
isolated peak, — can only die. Mr. Mulford says,[1]
"When Caius Marcius turns to the crowd in Rome
and denounces them as the detached and disorganized rabble, in whom there is nothing of the organic
unity of the people, the disdain of the Roman is
in the words, ' Go, get you home, you fragments! "
But how is it with the disdainful patrician himself?
Does not this very disdain cut *him* off from communion with his fellow-citizens, and is not there
the beginning of his own fragmentary split? The
patrician was no more the nation than the mobo-
cratic citizen. Had this rabble joined in a body
the Volscian host, where would have been the nation? Coriolanus joined it, and the nation still lived;
he was but a "fragment," and so he perished.

At that period of regal flattery, of royal absolutism, of adulating homage, Shakspeare speaks the
word that pierces through the high-flown forms and
reveals man as he is in himself. No wonder that
Voltaire is disgusted with a poet who can make a

---

[1] The Nation, p. 10.

queen say of herself, when addressed in deepest grief by her attendant as empress, —

> " No more, but e'en a woman; and commanded
> By such poor passion as the maid that milks,
> And does the meanest chares." [1]

In that age, when the idea of man as man had found no embodiment in word even, when human rights were nothing, and privilege and rank were all, Shakspeare makes his king say, — and from the mouth of a king the expression would easily escape comment: " The king is but a man, as I am; the violet smells to him as it doth to me; all his senses have but human conditions." And that well-known passage, since become a commonplace in the mouths of all, but then a strange sound of humanity pleading for the recognition of oneness: " Hath not a Jew eyes? Hath not a Jew hands, organs, senses, affections, passions? "

Since that time this " glittering generality " has become officially proclaimed; but almost all believe it to be only some flickering from the blaze of the nether pit, or some artificial light, electric or otherwise, which now flares up dazzlingly, and now leaves a blacker darkness as it flickers; and that at any rate, it will be totally extinguished before the clock strikes twelve. Few believe in it as the sun about which all the planets of this our social existence are turning, and which is to work out revolu-

---

[1] Antony and Cleopatra, act iv. scene 15.

tions greater than ever science or philosophy has dreamed. The true manhood of man is the problem that is to be solved; to this every discovery in science, every stroke of the steam-engine, every added means of education, every beat of the great human heart, is advancing from hour to hour.

That a nation is a living organism, Shakspeare's clear conception becomes more and more manifest; and if it is a real, organic form, one part cannot be turned from or hindered in its proper function without the entire organism being thereby affected. As our philosophic poet says, —

> " Let our finger ache, and it indues
> Our healthful members even to that sense
> Of pain."

Social effort, to-day, is based upon this fundamental truth, — the oneness of humanity as a living organism. Says a careful thinker,[1] " Not each nation only, but the whole human society, *under the conditions which now prevail*, is a vast organism, a body of many members with a mutual life." In Shakspeare's day it was not possible to see this organic life of the human race, for the present conditions did not exist. But the organic life of a nation Shakspeare did see, and he unfolded it with wonderful clearness.

In 1825, in his " Nouveau Christianisme," Saint-Simon advanced this ethical statement as the *résumé* of the teachings of Christ: " All should labor

[6] Inquiry into Socialism. By T. Kirkup. P. xxiv.

for the development, material, moral, and intellectual, of the lowest and poorest class." And this
would seem to be the nearest expression of that
apparent paradox uttered by Jesus, that if the feet,
the lowest part, were right, all would be right; and
that whoso ministered to the lowest and least ministered to him, the highest of all.

## XIV.

## THE COMMON REASON IN SOCIAL REFORMS.

THE principle of social progress may be formulated in these words : It is to give the *common reason* free play in the family, the school, the Church, and the State. All advance has been in this direction. If we look at the past, we shall see that the great secret of all blundering, all harmful legislation has been the endeavor to promote some private and partial end; to carry out measures to increase the prosperity of some one class or clique, some special order, in which the good only of some one part of society was supposed to be wrapped up. Hence the greater part of legislation, to-day, should aim at the removal of those restrictions which in the past have been imposed upon the many in the interest of the few, — in other words, to promote the highest good of the whole body politic.

Plato, with no conscious limitation of view in order to secure exclusive advantages to a special class, but to secure what he thought was for the highest benefit of the commonwealth, ordained that there should be a servile class, and that laborers and artisans should not be regarded as citizens, or have the rights of citizens. Such also was the view of Aristotle in his model State. Not until the American democratic State was established, did the essential manhood of *every* man become the basis of all legislation and all political arrangements. It was the victory of the common reason all along the line of man's relation to the State, and the State's relation to man.

But let us look at the real meaning of this term, " common reason," which is something more than what is ordinarily called common-sense. Buckle says that " every step in the progress of science is a contradiction to common-sense." He means that science is continually reversing the appearance of things to the senses; and so it is. If we take the testimony of the eye alone, the sun goes round the earth; the moon is as large as the sun; the sky is a dome over our heads; and the city-boss the very mainspring of all political movement. But this is only the appearance to the senses, until the intellect corrects it, and gives us an insight into the true relations of things in the material and social world.

The *communis sensus* — better named the " common reason " — is the verdict made up not by one faculty alone. If there is something else that enters into Nature and life than the impression made upon the senses, then that something else must be called into play before a true judgment can be pronounced. There *is* something else; and when there is the *consensus*, or agreement, of all the human faculties, then is common-sense exercised. To limit it to what commends itself to

vulgar eye, ear, and touch is to violate the very
conditions of its existence at all. It is the harmonious adjustment of all the faculties in the acknowledgment of the real fact.

Man has senses, by which he takes cognizance
of external things; he has understanding, by which
they are arranged in orderly sequence and depen-
dence; he has moral perception, by which the relative value and different relations to what is useful
and beneficial are established; he has also spiritual
perception, by which all these are conjoined and
subordinated in obedience to a pervading spirit of
wisdom and love, — and the harmonious expression
of all these faculties is common-sense, or the 'vox
Dei.' If any one takes precedence, no matter how
authoritative be the expression, the universality
or commonness fails. The voice of a majority,
however large, if it is the voice of a particular
faculty alone, is one-sided, partial, disorderly, — *vox
Diaboli*, not *vox Dei*. A people includes, repre-
sentatively, all these faculties; and if any one pre-
dominate, whether the priesthood or the masses,
the scholars or the artisans, there is distraction
and disorder. There are estates of the realm, and
no one estate must govern exclusively. How the
first estate governed was shown before the French
Revolution; and how the third, after its outbreak.
Every parliament or congress or general assembly
is an attempt to get at the *consensus communis* of
the entire body of the nation.

That there is a collective wisdom far superior to

that of the individual judgment is affirmed by that extraordinary professor of common-sense, Aristotle, who says in the third book of his " Politics ": —

"The people at large, how contemptible soever they may appear when taken individually, are yet, when collectively considered, not perhaps unworthy of sovereignty. It is a common remark that those entertainments where each man sends the dish most agreeable to his own palate, are preferable to those furnished by the most sumptuous delicacy of individuals. The people at large are admitted to be the best judges of music and poetry. The general taste is thus acknowledged to be better than that of the few, or of any one man however skilful. The excellences of that complex body the Public may sometimes surpass those of the most accomplished prince, or of the most virtuous counsel."

But from this " Public " Aristotle would carefully exclude all laborers and artisans!

In every day individual life, there is in each one of us what may·be called an invisible parliament or congress of representatives from every department, — even from the remotest part of body and soul, — to enact laws, issue proclamations, devise ways and means, ascertain our revenue, and regulate our expenses. This parliament of faculties presides over all our thoughts, yet it is embodied in no formal statement; it is back of all our conscious will, yet compels no individual conviction; it mingles in every exercise of judgment and reason, yet has no visible tribunal; its verdict is final, yet it is enacted

in no formal statute. It is the presence of what may
be called the common or universal reason. As the
spiritual Fénelon says: "It is not myself, for it re-
proves and corrects me against my will. This reason
is the rule of my reason; and from this every wise
man is instructed."

This also is the great rule not only for the individual, but for the social order and common life. In
social order, neither anarchy nor despotism can endure, but each is modified and restrained by this con-
trolling influence. Amidst oscillations from abnormal tastes and one-sided tendencies, this omnipotent
element asserts itself, bringing chaotic strivings into harmonious adjustment. As the atmosphere is
always tending to purify itself, and come into the
condition of relative proportion of gases needed for
sound lungs and healthy breathing, so in the social
world the moist humors are absorbed, the chill mists
are scattered, the acids diluted, and effervescing
substances compounded into neutral salts, while the
work of reaction and ebullition is never at an end.
Parties and sects are bent upon making every man
breathe pure oxygen, but Nature knows better than
that. She tolerates for long no exclusive systems,
laughs at all panaceas, and quietly sets her veto on
all perpetual motions. Science would reduce the
world to a laboratory of crucibles, retorts, and material atoms, while piety would make it a cell for
monkish asceticism. The intellect would analyze,
dissect, and question without end, while faith would
accept everything, believing the more fervently as

the incredibility increases. But there is a regulating principle which permits no violent tendency to continue unobstructed, and which when the machine revolves too rapidly for safety shuts off the steam, — balancing a Luther with a Loyola, conservatives with reformers, eyes looking towards the sunset with eyes gazing into the brightening dawn.

In education, see how speedily extreme theories are brought to a level and absorbed into the general circulation, all the good being assimilated as nutriment into the system. Heated brains and abnormal temperaments, wild philanthropists and zealous theorists broach their one-sided projects, and then are heard of no more. But much that is good remains, and enters into life. At one time it is all study of the languages, and at another of science; now all must be play, and now all hard work; now everything must be made plain, and now stated only in barest outline; now all must be lecture, and now all lesson. A better culture is demanded for the body, a better training for the physical man. Then theorists start up with their special systems, enthusiasts of one idea follow out their peculiar methods; and soon each falls into partial neglect. Base-ball becomes a professional knack; foot-ball, a brutal melée of muscle and brawn; rowing, an unnatural training of a few, and a competitive straining even to complete organic collapse. But step by step, steadily and surely, the young are brought upon a higher plane, the highest thought is enlisted in discovering the best methods of training, and the results of varied experiences are diffused and made available. In other words, the invisible regulator, the common reason, has the final say.

This final dictum of the common reason prevails in some cases where we should scarcely expect to see it. Not with impunity can any one clique or party, any one sect or school, claim to be the exclusive depositaries of truth. To assert such a claim is to become separate from humanity, and to cut oneself off from the universal inspiration. This may be seen in what appear, at first sight, to be provinces the farthest removed from any such danger. Said once a learned solicitor-general of England, in the House of Commons, in regard to law reform: "I must warn the House, if they attempt legal reforms, that they must not allow lawyer after lawyer to get up and tell them that they are not capable of understanding the subject. They might depend upon it that if they could not reduce a legal proposition to the plain principles of common-sense comprehensible to persons of ordinary intelligence, the defect was that it was a technical system invented for the creation of costs, and not to promote the administration of justice." This is in harmony with what an eminent professor of jurisprudence (Professor Grote) says: "Law is the *public reason* of a society participated in, more or less, by the mass of individuals."

We may say, indeed, of all sciences, — except those involving the higher mathematics, — that if they cannot be reduced to universal principles comprehensible to sound minds and upright hearts, they are but conventional and technical terminologies, which will soon be superseded. For science does not contradict, it formulates, facts according to the principles of the common reason. It confirms and establishes them on an immovable basis; it shows order in the apparent disorder. As a philosophical observer, in describing the mer-de-glace at Chamouni, says, —

" At first the ice presented an appearance of utter confusion ; but we soon reached a position where the mechanical conditions of the glacier revealed themselves, and where we might learn — had we not known it before — that confusion is merely the unknown mixture of laws, and becomes order and beauty when we rise to their comprehension.

This is the " harmony not understood," which belongs to the entire created universe in its minutest part. This is the Cosmos, or beautiful order, which if science does not give us, it gives us nothing really worth having. But it does always end in establishing for us what was already prophesied in the higher intuitions, — in the demand for order, symmetry, law.

Look at what we call law. The State passes certain laws, — for what professed end? To carry out the ends of justice, — that is, to carry out ends which have their existence, their foundation, in something which precedes the laws, and which calls them into being. The law, therefore, does not create justice; but justice creates the law, of which it is supposed to be the embodiment. Justice is the divine reality, and abides in the souls of those who seek to make it a concrete, actual thing. Back of all State enactments is that justice which is universal and divine, which gives them their justification and their force. A calm, philosophic observer says of the legislation of Great Britain at the present time, —

"The revolution which is being effected in due course of law is the gradual but complete transference of the source of legislation from the select ruling portion of society to the whole body of the people. Instead of law, as of old, flowing down from king, lords, and commons to the people, law is now impelled in an upward flow from the people to the commons, lords, and monarch." [1]

So it is with the higher philosophy. "True philosophy," it has been said, "accepts, as given, the great and indestructible convictions of our race, and the language in which these are expressed; and in place of denying or obliterating them, she endeavors rationally to explain and justify them." [2] Such is the work of philosophy to-day in every department, — not rudely sneering or denying, but seeking those broader statements which underlie every universal conviction from the earliest historic times. The old philosopher Heraclitus said that "it behooves us all to follow the common reason of the

---

[1] The Political Life of our Time. By D. Nichol. Vol. ii. p. 336.
[2] Blackwood's Magazine, April, 1838, — "Consciousness."

world" rather than private and individual idiosyncracies; and this is true in art, in literature, in every sphere in which universal principles of truth and beauty manifest themselves. The final verdict in the ages is made up from the consensus of those who are exponents of this universal wisdom, or reason.

Goethe uttered many a maxim pregnant with wisdom, but nothing wiser than when he said, "The best way to preserve our common-sense is to live in the universal way with multitudes of men." The anchorite and the nun become exceptional, and they pay the penalty. The martyrs are not always martyrs to truth and righteousness, but often to their own one-sided interpretation of truth, and sometimes to their own self-assertion and self-conceit. It is a nice line that separates the pure impersonal devotion to principle from the love of singularity, the desire for self-prominence and self-extension. Pretentious vanity, exclusive assumption, even under the garb of single-minded service, gets persistently rebuffed, and wonders why its claims are so coldly met or contemptuously rejected. Why should such well-meaning exertion and earnest good-will not meet with a better reward? The sufferer does not see; for he does not perceive that his own atmosphere envelopes those with whom he comes in contact, and that this atmosphere is one of offensive personal assumption, perhaps of exclusiveness and contempt. We used to hear, more than we do to-day, the woman earnest for reform jeered at as strong-minded; and charges

were made as to the color of her stockings, whenever a woman was suspected of knowing a little
more than the average man.  I have sometimes tried
to think that this was the growling way which some
men had of expressing their belief that the highest
womanly excellence is a loving heart predominat-
ing every other faculty, original or acquired.  The
good masculine souls did not want the fair creatures
to become "*too* good for human nature's daily food."
It was not for woman's interest, you know, and women would be the greatest sufferers from it in the
long run!  Well, it is a woman who gives this
charming description of Mrs. Somerville, as " not
dwelling aloof from common men and women, but
throwing herself into the interests of those around
her, conversing with each in his or her own way;
being the kindest and pleasantest member of society, — a sad stone of stumbling to those who
delight to depict that heraldic creature 'the strong-
minded female,' and to those who have established
it as a fact that the knowledge of Euclid is incompatible with the domestic affections."

In regard to the social relations and duties of
woman, common reason has had, at last, something
to say.  It seems now so much a matter of course
for men and women to sit together, study together,
and work together, that we forget from what she
has been rescued, in spite of the protests of the
*colossal* intellects and the *great* minds in Church
and State, — that " chosen remnant " of the great
and good, so dear to Matthew Arnold's heart.  Why,

the great General Assembly of the Church of Scotland, no longer ago than 1649, passed a law that all women must sit together, and sit " laigh " in the kirk. But as sitting " low " was found conducive to a comfortable nap, " a church officer was ordered to go through the church with a long pole, to remove the plaids from the heads of all women, whether wives or maids." The New England tithing-man, who was the terror of boys and girls, had thus a very respectable ancestry, and was not the native growth of puritanic Massachusetts or Connecticut. Of course, if all the women are put away by themselves, and all the boys by themselves, they must have special legislation to meet their special cases; but come down to the hard pan of common reason, and no legislation whatever is needed.

In whatever direction we look, then, we see that it is fidelity to universal principles that constitutes real greatness and worth. In these only are all men at home. As he gives expression to these, the poet meets the deepest response from the hearts of his fellows; and as the exponent of these, men crown him king, and own themselves his obedient subjects. The orator utters that which all were waiting to hear, and wanting to express. The heroism, the wisdom, the truth is theirs also, and they breathe one common air. His word is power, because he appeals to the universal heart. He stands there to show off no individual graces or personal excellences or superior wit.   He gives up his own life, and so receives the life of all.   True, true everywhere is that utterance of Fichte, —

"Whatever a man may do, so long as he does it *from* himself, *by* himself, and *through* his own counsel, it is vain, and will sink to nothing.   All things new, great, and beautiful which have appeared in the world since its beginning, and those which will appear until its end, have appeared and will appear through the divine or [common-human] idea."

The pet notion, the peculiar theory, however grand, however expressive of personal and individual power, comes to nought.   That which embodies the ideas of beauty, of justice, of wisdom which are in all souls must endure so long as that which inspires them, and that from which they draw, continues to endure.   "It is characteristic of the highest truth," says one, "to be accessible to common minds, and inaccessible only to ambitious ones." [1]

Here, now, we strike the key-note of Shakspeare's greatness and lasting power.   He has no idiosyncracy, no favorite string, no recurring strain from his own individual likes and dislikes; no pet theory of man or woman; no special cause or doctrine to advocate, whether in Church or State.   He gives every one a chance to speak through him, as if he were simply the conduit for his or her individual being.   Hence he is the

[1] The Secret of Swedenborg.   By Henry James.

interpreter of humanity and not of any particular class or clique, or of odd specimens of men and women. He hits the golden mean. Mr. Blackie sums up the ethics of Aristotle thus: —

" Virtue is a medium, a balance, a proportion, a symmetry, a harmony, a nice adjustment of the force of each part in reference to the calculated action of the whole."

Now, Shakspeare makes the disturbance of this balance, this harmony, the theme of all his tragedy, whether as applied to the general State, the Commonwealth, or that individual State, that private common-weal of which each man is a citizen, and in which he ought to rule. To preserve this balance is the secret of all happiness, of all true well-being. "It is no mean happiness to be seated in the mean; superfluity comes sooner by white hairs, but competency lives longer," — this is the leading theme, with infinite variations.

This wisdom comes not from any intellectual elevation, but from a dramatic sympathy with humanity in its various developments. It is the ethics which lives in those proverbs that grow up, one knows not how or where, in the heart of the people, and finds expression in the maxim that embodies the experience of entire generations. Its power is in its universality and its commonness. It is the wisdom of all, — that *communis sensus* which, after all, is the highest and the last appeal. No man can be wiser than humanity; and as the exponent of

18

this purely human, universal (and because human and universal, also divine) wisdom, Shakspeare remains unreached and alone.

In admitting this, Rümelin,[1] who loses no opportunity to depreciate Shakspeare, really concedes to him, while depreciating him, the highest claim as a moralist; and he can but grant the vast superiority of Shakspeare, in this respect, over Schiller and Goethe. " Their maxims," he says, " occupy a different sphere; and Goethe's, especially, rest upon an individual point of view wholly foreign from the folk-wisdom. In Shakspeare, on the contrary, we perceive a noteworthy trait of congeniality with this spirit of the people, not in any one peculiar direction, but in that wisdom as a whole." What greater praise could be given to Shakspeare's ethical genius?

It is indeed worth the while to study this body of natural divinity, as it may be called, wherein the concentrated wisdom of humanity lives in forms to which the highest intuitive perception, united with the most genial poetic power, has given an enduring embodiment. These thickly strewn sayings sound often like quoted proverbs, but they are from Shakspeare's own mint; as, —

" Thrift is blessing, if men steal it not."
" To hear with eyes belongs to love's fine wit."
" Will is deaf, and heeds no heedful friends."
" It is an heretic that makes the fire, not he which burns in 't."

[1] RÜMELIN : *Shakspeare Studien*, p. 166.

" Wishers were ever fools."

" In poison there is physic."

" Good words are better than bad strokes."

" He that loves to be flattered is worthy of the flatterer."

> " There is some soul of goodness in things evil,
> Would men observingly distil it out."

> > " Love yourself ; and in that love,
> Not unconsidered leave your honor."

" Best men are moulded out of faults."

" They love not poison that do poison need."

Thousands of like significance could be quoted, — all springing from the character, the time, the place, and the occasion, and all sounding as if the spirit of human wisdom itself had brooded for generations over the utterance.

We are often repelled when these representations of dramatic power are made, by the extravagant claims that are set up for the individual man, William Shakspeare, — as if he must have been himself so very wise and so very good and so very great in his own personal character and life. But his real value to us is that he could throw himself, such as he was, into every form that he summoned into his presence. His own self was merged for the time in the self of another, and by losing himself he gained humanity. He carried into manhood that faculty which belongs to the child, — " the six years' darling of a pigmy size."

> " See at his feet some little plan or chart,
> Some fragment from his dream of human life,

> Shaped by himself with newly-learnèd art, —
> A wedding or a festival,
> A mourning or a funeral.
> And this hath now his heart,
> And unto this he frames his song;
> Then will he fit his tongue
> To dialogues of business, love, or strife.
> But it will not be long
> Ere this be thrown aside,
> And with new joy and pride
> The little actor cons another part,
> Filling from time to time his humorous stage
> With all the persons down to palsied age,
> That Life brings with her in her equipage, —
> As if his whole vocation
> Were endless imitation."

That free joy and sympathy with every form of being; that abandonment to the impression of Nature and life which gave rise to mythology, and which is the soul of all the creations of every child, — this gave us the Shakspearian drama, with all its lessons of the truth that lies at the basis of every fact and of every emotion.

Because of the influence of this common reason, we find that in literature the best survives; that evermore there is a winnowing process going on by which the solid grain is saved, and the dust and chaff and lighter matter are sent whirling into the great cavern of forgetfulness, never again to mislead or vex human souls. What is this grand winnowing machine on which there is no patent for exclusive use, and from which there is no possible way of escape? Time, you say. But

time is only the name given to a succession of
changes. There is no such entity as time; but
there is a *communis sensus*, a divine reason, immanent in human things and human souls, which
forever acts, and from which there is no appeal.

This common reason of the world is expressed,
too, in its proverbs, which sound the entire gamut
of human experience. In the derivation of the
word " proverb," there is the recognition of this relation to a universal wisdom. When a man uses
such a saying, he uses *pro verbo* (instead of his *own*
word) every man's word: he does not carry his
own special lantern, but opens a shutter and lets in
the sunlight; he merges self in the all-comprehend-
ing self of humanity; he utters not his individual
truth, but the conviction of his fellows. So, too,
with the legends, the sagas, the mythologies of all
nations: they are not the product of a few wise
heads, select literary students, or rare scholars,
but the product of a Universal Intelligence, whose
depths no man has sounded, — waifs cast upon the
shore by the all-surrounding ocean of truth; revelations made by a general daylight, not by any
number of coruscating meteors or winking stars.

This *communis sensus*, then, this divine reason in
the community, is the real source of all social
development; and, as it is trusted to, it gives a
cheering confidence in the accomplishment, not
perhaps of our short-sighted schemes, but of all the
purposes of higher good that we cherish for ourselves and our fellow-men. The fine scholar trusts

in the few trained souls and in the chosen few.
" The mass of the people," says one of England's
ripest scholars, " look for guidance in political as
in other matters to their natural social leaders, to
their aristocracy. Any government founded on the
idea that people ever do, or ever can, govern themselves is a delusion." But what shall we poor
souls do who have no aristocracy? My social
leader is he who will reveal to me the truth, and
awaken within me any dormant power. The light
by which I see, if I see at all, comes to me not
from any special training; but it has illumined and
judged and set its seal of approval or condemnation upon every book, every teacher, every word.
And this light is in *me* because it is in every man;
and therefore when I think of this great American
nation, of which I also am glad to be a part, I say of
it what a Catholic lady, a member of the French
nobility, once said of the French nation in one of
its political crises, —

" This people has shown itself so amenable to reason
in so many difficult circumstances, that I believe in its
true progress. All the confidence I have rests on this
public reason, which has no proper name of its own, but
which we have seen concentrate in itself alone resolution
and strength."

The people to get only the guidance which comes
from their natural leaders! But what if this superior position and select training are the very obstacles which shut these leaders' eyes and close their

ears? Why is it that so many, with every advantage of birth and education, fail to speak the right word when any crisis comes, and thus cease to be the leaders of men? It is because they are out of that main current which runs onward to the open sea, and every little eddy whirls them about and turns them aside. Out of the steadily blowing trade-wind, the stateliest ship must lie with flapping sails and groaning timbers in the region of baffling winds or unchanging calm, while the fleets of little boats speed along to their destined haven. Napoleon the First was a wonderful genius; but the genius of humanity is more wonderful than he. That prison of isolated rock in mid-ocean was the true symbol of his real isolation from the great world of human tendencies and social needs. What an awful revelation, yet with such pure unconsciousness of what its real meaning was, is that question of his: "Is not the statesman wholly an *eccentric* personage, always alone by himself, — he on one side, and the world on the other?" Egoism arising almost to sublimity! Contrast it with the utterance, "Yet am I not alone, for the Father [the ALL] is with me!" All the forces of love and truth are working with him, working through him, and working for him.

Another illustration is given us in a great genius before whose power we have all bowed, and whose words have been like the rustling winds in the forest of pines, — Mr. Ruskin. He asks with all imaginable naïveté, —

" How it is that well educated princes, who ought to be of all gentlemen the gentlest, and of all nobles the most generous, and whose title of royalty means only their function of doing every man 'right;' how it is that these, throughout history, should so rarely pronounce themselves on the side of the poor and of justice; how it comes to pass that a captain will die with his passengers, and leaning over the gunwale give the departing boat its course; but that a king will not usually die *with*, much less *for*, HIS passengers, thinking it rather incumbent on them, in any number, to die for *him*, — think, I beseech you, of the wonder of this!"

Yes, let us think of it. Who are these princes and kings? Persons cut off from any vital connection with the rest of humanity. There was a time when Shakspeare could make his king say, — a king who *was* ready to die with and for his fellow-Englishmen, — "The king, too, is a man like you." But is it any wonder that when his office has become merely a perfunctory one, when all his virtue consists in his aloofness from the common herd, and when from the earliest moment he has been taught that he is of better stuff than other men, — is it any wonder that he should feel it incumbent on him to preserve by all means that delicate and precious porcelain, while the coarse clay-pots may look out for themselves? To-day something else besides the accident of birth determines who shall govern the ship, the factory, the railway, and the church. How would the divine right of birth answer here?

Then, further, it is treason and disloyalty to refuse

to serve the king! But is it not equally treason and disloyalty for the king not to serve the people? Yet how can he serve them when a different life-stream flows through his veins ? — for which difference he must pay the penalty. Mr. Ruskin does not see why a poor king should be excused, because Mr. Ruskin himself has no belief in the common reason of humanity, but only in the institutions of the past. He once gave a fine definition of a noble war: " A noble war is one waged simply for the defence of the country in which we were born, and for the maintenance and execution of her laws, by whomsoever threatened or defied." Very good; but how was it, dear Critic, that you left no occasion unimproved to scoff at our country when she poured out her treasure and her blood to maintain and to execute her laws, threatened and defied? Why was your vision then darkened? Alas! you believed in what you called the divine right of born gentlemen, not in the human right of God-inspired men; you believed in the privileged greatness of the few, not in the might of all. You had no belief in the people as the instrument of that wondrous power which evermore sweeps over its trembling strings!

More wonderful than even the most wonderful visionary dreams will be the accomplished facts, if the universal principles of justice, order, and human sympathies are ever fully embodied in the everyday life and work, — just as the wonders of steam, of the magnet, and of electricity now surpass the wildest fancies of the Arabian Nights. Social progress has but just begun; for the common reason of humanity being hitherto in abeyance, men have never yet combined their efforts for the happiness and well-being of all.

But the trend of all history is in that direction. The energy and science and practical skill of the human race are to be employed in the service of common reason, if not of philanthropy; and then will be more than realized the most enthusiastic dreams of social welfare. Read the account of some Woolwich arsenal with its hundred spreading acres; its sixty steam-engines; its miles of shafting; its running gear for a thousand complicated machines; its ten thousand workmen, all busy in making engines of ruin, — engines to be used for destroying human life and laying waste the results of human industry, — and say what shall come to pass when there shall be the combined and scientific adaptation of skill and machinery to the benefit, and not to the harm, of the human family!

Most heartily do we agree with Professor Jowett, the learned translator of Plato and of Aristotle, that "there is no absurdity in expecting that the mass of mankind having the power in their own hands, and becoming enlightened about the higher possibilities of human life, when they come to see how much more is attainable for all than is at present the possession of a favored few, may pursue the common interest with an intelligence and persistency which the world has not yet seen."

# XV.

## HISTORY AS DEVELOPMENT.

" WHAT is it," says the Chevalier Bunsen, " to write a chapter of the universal history of mankind but to recompose a canto of that most sacred epic of which God is the poet, humanity the hero, and the historian the interpreter ?" What other than this can history be if the life of humanity is an unfolding of a divine spirit? For the natural world is no more a transcript of divine thought than is the social world, all whose parts are streamlets running into the one ocean of universal history. We may call this poem of history an epic or a drama: as a serene past, it is the former; as acted in the present, it is the latter. *It*, no less than material phenomena, is the revelation of an infinite variety of facts and processes, under which lie unity, order, and progressive life.

History is of value, then, as being the record of the spiritual or infinite element in humanity. Just as everything in the natural world has life so far as in some individual form it expresses the universal life, so every human being has life so far as in some individual form *he* embodies the universal life. This universal life finds its highest expression in society; that is, in laws, arts, business, and various social in-

stitutions.  If there were no recorded history, there
could be no continuity of social life and no consciousness of a higher destiny.  Historical development is simply man's growth in individuality and
freedom.  In an Oriental despotism there is but
little individuality; all look alike and act alike, as a
school of herring or a herd of buffaloes.  At the
opposite extreme is a true democracy, where each
man is distinctly himself, and in obeying the universal will obeys consciously the common reason embodied in his own thought.

In the so-called democracies of Greece and Rome
and the Italian cities, there was nothing like the form
of society which we have arrived at to-day.  It is
futile to point to them now, and say that we have
no more surety of surviving than they.  The democracies of the past were but another form of external government; they were not the developments
of the spiritual nature of man, becoming embodied
in the only form adapted to inherent, living powers.
That our form of government secures to us the most
and the greatest material advantages, is not the chief
claim which it should have in our eyes: while it
does this, it does infinitely more.  But if we could
have ten times the material good secured to us by
arrangements in which we had no participation, we
should reject such an external bountifulness; for its
price would be our manhood and our free consciousness, — in other words, of our capacity for growth
and indefinite progress.  To be complete up to a
certain point, and to have this completeness formed

for us from without, would be to reduce us to the
range of mere animal instinct; and *there* we should
remain fixed forever. But history shows us that
man has forever been making mistakes, — sad mistakes, foolish mistakes, wicked mistakes, — yet that
he has had the ability to correct these mistakes, to
become as it were a new creature, alive with the life
of the creative spirit. This is the only progress; and
this is the process unfolded in history.

As simply a form of repressive government to im-
pose regulations from without, to restrain and direct
men, a democratic form of government may easily
be the poorest of all forms. But as the embodiment of the conscious reason abiding in the social
body and seeking an expression for itself, a democratic form is the only fitting one. Whatever social
changes may be needed to embody perfectly the
universal life, those changes will come, must come;
for the divine in man must find a development in
every word and work. The infinite ocean must flow
into every creek, inlet, harbor, and bay. All the
spheres of education, law, art, and industry must
become organic forms of harmonious life.

In this light of historical development, all the socialistic plans must be looked upon as utterly inad-
equate and incomplete, because they cut away the
very veins and sinews through which man is related
to the universal life; they destroy individuality and
freedom; they reduce men and women to an indis-
tinguishable mass. They would do *for* man and
*over* man what must be done by him and through

him.   Yet every socialistic demand is a recurring
admonition that we are what history shows us to
be, — members of one common body, receivers of
one divine life.

For thousands of years the human race has been
toiling, scheming, thinking, aspiring, embodying as
it could, from day to day, its visions and its plans.
In the social world have been contests as great,
struggles as vast, as have ever taken place in the
natural and physical universe.  Is any one man
adequate to say what shall be the crystallization
to take place from this mingling of substances?
Each of us can imagine some state of things
which should be without this annoyance or that
pain, in which there should be no disease, no sorrow, no ill, — for to dream is the easiest of things.
Looked at aright, the history of humanity is the
story of aspiration rather than of accomplishment.
What finally has been accomplished has been far
different from what often was aimed at, and far
grander than was ever dreamed.  Great Britain
started a commercial company to gather in the ru-
pees of India, and now a vast empire is committed
to her guidance and her rule.  Our forefathers
thought to find a place where they could worship
unmolested, and build up, after their own ideal pattern, a little vestibule to heaven; but an indwelling
spirit, wiser and more far-seeing than all, thwarted
their narrow plans, and built up this Western temple,
in which all the creeds of Christendom and Heathen-
dom alike should find a home.

Saint-Simon had his dream of an industrial society with its chief, whose legitimate authority all
would acknowledge because he was confessedly the
chief, and whom all would freely obey because all
held him in love; where perfect order would reign,
and no workman be without guidance and help;
where all should have the necessary tools, and all
be employed in congenial work; where one should
no longer use another as an instrument to his
own private good, but all should seek to beautify
the earth by their united labors, and to make all the
riches of the earth a common inheritance. Though
the particular form which that dream assumed may
be an illusion, and its fulfilment cannot come in the
way that was dreamed of, yet by all the sacred pages
of the past history of our race, the living spirit of
humanity shall triumph in a way that is infinitely
beyond man's limited schemes.

There is no short cut to establish permanently
even the highest and most perfect form of political
and social life. Progress is neither in a straight
line nor in a circle returning to the same point; it
is a spiral movement, so that when you seem to be
going the same round you are really on a higher
plane. Though in the natural world you may not
be able to say where is the boundary line between
mineral and plant, between plant and animal, between animal and man, each stage of organic
life is on a higher plane than the preceding, and
there is an advance from the simpler to the more
complex forms.

So in humanity itself there is the elimination, step by step, of what belonged to a lower stage of development; and though there may be carried along with the advance many of the rudimentary organs, they have ceased to dominate the life or make essential a special method of existence. Outgrown shells are left behind; useless appendages are dropped. Feudalism was once the best form in which humanity could find expression for its needs; it was a natural, orderly, and beneficent crystallization of the desires, hopes, and ideals of the time; hamlet and village sheltered themselves under the protection of castle and feudal lord. But when trade and commerce grew up, when the middle classes asserted their right to be, the castle became a den of robbers, an incubus upon the earth. So monastic institutions, — the natural and spontaneous product of social and spiritual needs in special conditions, — were once a blessing and were blessed. But that peculiar need has passed away, and monastic walls and monastic rules remain only to warp and pervert man's higher aspirations, — to witness useless mortifications, half-believing prayers, and silent curses of dehumanized devotees. When privileged classes or orders only suck up the life-blood of humanity, when they render no service in return, they must yield their place; for to retain the privileges and shirk the price by which alone they were bestowed, what is that?

Service to humanity is the condition of every form of embodiment in social life. Through priest

and lord, through merchant and mechanic, through
soldier and artist, humanity seeks to unfold its own
inner life, its indwelling capacities of love and wisdom. Hence there must be many attempts before
the final success; there must be defeats before any
great victory is attained. That his muscles should
be made strong is the real prize that the gymnast
wins; that his moral powers should be unfolded is
worth more to a true man than any external success; and that humanity should have heroes, martyrs, and saints is better than selfish comfort and
bestial content. Therefore the way of progress is
not strewn with flowers; the ascent is steep, the
friendly stars seem hidden. Great sacrifices to be
made call forth the great souls to make them. Innumerable lives must pay the price of victory; and,
as Guizot says, " it is only after an unknown number
of unrecorded labors, after a host of noble hearts
have succumbed in discouragement, convinced that
the cause is lost, — it is then only that the cause
triumphs."

Men sometimes see their best efforts thwarted,
and the good that has been sought for with infinite toil seized upon as a means of harm. The
liberty for which pure hearts labored and prayed
is sometimes turned into license; the truth hailed
as the dawn of some glorious day becomes a thick
pall over the midday sky; the banner on which pure
hands have wrought, which tears have consecrated,
and the morning light has seen thrown out joyously
to the breeze, is borne aloft at evening by the

advancing hosts of anarchy and crime. But has naught been gained? Has not defeat been the means to a success greater than was at first dreamed of?

To the physical world great cycles of ages alone suffice for some new stage of growth; and why be impatient for the moral and social world? Ideal truths belong to a realm of infinity; and what may be the special good accomplished through this or that means no human insight can determine. One man's failure may be as needful as another's success. He who always succeeds in what he attempts may be sure that in his attempts no grand ideal purpose is involved. It is noble to fail in some great cause; it is noble to fail where one's aim is so high that one short life is all insufficient to realize it in his human environment; it is divine to have aspirations so great and principles so broad that only ages of the coming time shall look upon them as accomplished facts. But has any good cause ever failed? In one place and at one time it may seem to have failed, to have died and been buried. But no man and no people have labored for good utterly to no purpose. When the flower perishes, the seed is scattered abroad and the harvest springs up, though perhaps in distant lands. "How I love," says Alfred Vaughan, "to find examples of that consoling truth that no well-meant effort for God and man can ever really die! that the relics of vanished, vanquished endeavors are gathered up and conserved, and by the spiritual chemistry of

Providence are transformed into a new life in a
new age ! "

There is a transmigration of ideas, if not of separate souls. Though institutions die, that which they
were meant to embody still lives. Forms of civilized life perish ; but the soul which *informed* them
inspires new institutions, new systems of polity, new
philosophies, new customs and arts. Bravery, royalty, thought, faith, do not die with the knight, the
king, the philosopher, the monk, in whom each once
found an adequate exponent. Cathedrals crumble
to dust and priesthoods disappear, but reverence
and love survive. The feudal castle is tumbled into
the moat, and the throne is consumed in fire ; but
order and law embody themselves in larger forms.
The real life-giving principle in every human organization — that which gave it birth and kept it sound
— does not die with the men, the institutions, but
disappears only to be manifest in some better embodiment, some more perfectly adapted form.

Pythagoras and Plato moulded the living principles of Oriental wisdom into Greek classic beauty
and practical use. The Roman Church shaped into
a mighty whole the spiritual secrets of Buddha and
Brahma, of Egypt and Greece, of Phœnicia and Palestine. The Protestant Reformation created a new
world for free, unlimited development of every seed
that has in it the germ of life. As the prophetic soul
of Milton saw, the people of England were transport-
ing in his day "a plant of more beneficial qualities
and more noble growth than that which Triptolemus

was reported to have carried from region to region."
And that we have such an inheritance of rich and
manifold elements from the past — all ages and all
generations — is the surest pledge of a grand development not hitherto attained.

Life has always been rich, potent, and assimilating as it has been the resultant of complex,
numerous, and manifold component elements. One
individual, one tribe, one nation, of itself and by
itself, has little capacity for growth and progress.
Hellas owed its fuller development to the variety
of its constituent germs ; Rome, to its power of
assimilating and incorporating different elements ;
England, to the movements resulting from the contests, the action and reaction, of races, classes, interests, and occupations. And America to-day is
projecting in colossal form what these display in
miniature. The very idea of universal history forces
itself upon us from our condition as a nation. What
a commingling here of all that mother earth has
produced of blood, language, religion, industry,
science, and art! Our national life is a heated furnace to melt into a glowing mass the rough ores
that are poured into its open mouth, to be hardened and tempered into steel. The number, the
diversity, the free play, the interaction, of physical,
social, and moral influences, — no one can imagine
it! Can the result be other than a human development broader than has ever before been witnessed?
A true cosmopolitanism must be the issue of a
variety of elements so rich and manifold, subordi-

nated and moulded as they all are by the one principle of individual manhood, the common atmosphere of freedom to think, to speak, to worship, and to vote.

Hitherto war, invasion, and trade have been the rude means by which the stagnant pools have been stirred and the incrusted surfaces have been broken up. But to-day the relation is more direct. There is action and reaction between the remotest parts of the globe. Each portion of the race begins to feel its need of all the others; each to be aware, in some way however faint and imperfect, that it can promote the prosperity of all by being faithful to its own peculiar service. That phrase " oneness of humanity" has been uttered. The spiritual philosopher proclaims that " the whole human race exists as one man before God." Daniel Webster said, from his position as a statesman: " Each nation has the same interest in the preservation of the laws of nations that each individual has in the preservation of the laws of his country." Never before could such a sentiment meet with such a universal response as now, when the broader the sentiment the more enthusiastic its reception. A common consciousness is awakened by the common life, and an event that deeply touches one people touches some chords of sympathy in every people's heart. Walls and barriers fall down; mysteries become open secrets; the wisdom of the wise is inherited by all; the results of industry and thought are brought to a common mart, and will be more and more freely

interchanged between people and people, — every
invention passing from mind to mind and from
hand to hand.

Does it indicate nothing that humanity now rises
above the horizon as the ideal of human souls? To
know man, his faculties, his wants, his hindrances,
and his helps, — this is education; to love him and
labor for him, — this is religion; to impart to him
beauty in every sphere of life, — this is art; to en-
rich him and add to his means of comfort and well-
being, — this is industry. From this ideal the stirring life of the present takes its tone, its direction,
its real force. Genius builds methods of education,
not rituals and elaborate ceremonials; arranges national exhibitions, not fields of golden cloth where
monarchs spend the income of their subjects; con-
structs palaces for the million, not luxurious abodes
for a king. It devises amelioration for human suffering, not splendid pageants of Oriental adoration.
The vital efficiency of every movement is in proportion to its enthronement of this ideal. The " cry
of the human " is not from some solitary dungeon,
or from some one grand martyr upon the cross;
it comes from the fields and the streets, from the
church and the workshop, from the college and from
legislative halls. The demand for the removal of
social hindrances, for a juster distribution of the
profits of industry, for universal education, for the
relief of suffering and want, is in conformity with
this ideal, — and so must receive a fitting response ; for no ideal that has inspired humanity

has ever yet failed of being actualized in outward
forms.

The change into a higher form of social life is
necessarily accompanied by the decay and death of
what has previously enshrined the aspirations and
hopes of man.   The night of an old civilization
seems to grow darker and darker just before the
dawning of a new, — recalling the old pious French
proverb, which says, " Patience ! it is when the demon has said his last word, that God speaks."   Perhaps an instinctive perception of this has placed the
birth-time of him in whom the " enthusiasm of humanity" was a ruling passion, and whose luminous
place in the history of our race marks a broad line
of division between the setting of old hopes and the
rising of new in the soul of man, in that season of
midwinter when the sun shines only with slanting
beams, when the daylight is shortest, and the frost-
bound forces of creative Nature seem asleep or dead.
A dark hour was that when thousands and tens of
thousands fled from Germany, England, and France ;
but it preceded the light of free institutions in this
western hemisphere.   When in our own country
overbearing power celebrated its crowning triumph
in the fugitive-slave law, the dawn of the day of
universal freedom was very near.   So in every age
the lesson is taught that only the surface changes,
while humanity abides forever, — gaining strength
from weakness, triumph from defeat !

There is always movement and change, even if it
be not always progress.   No more in the social than

in the natural world is there absolute rest. Even
when the eye seems to look out upon an unvarying
landscape, great alterations are taking place, — con-
tinents are forming, mountains are upheaving, oceans
are changing their bed, each particle of solid rock is
in motion, lakes are filling up, forests are growing,
deserts are becoming gardens, and prairies are becoming populous cities. The old is ever passing
away, and the new is emerging. The causes that
produce revolutions are ever at work; the earth-
quake is gathering force, the volcano is dying out.
So beliefs are becoming obsolete; power is changing
hands; new faiths are studding the firmament of
man's life. This continual movement in the universe Goethe thus enunciates : —

> " It must go on, creating, changing,
>     Through endless shapes forever ranging,
>     And rest we only *seem* to see.
>     The eternal lives through all revolving,
>     For all must ever keep dissolving
>     Would it continue still to be."

Cowper has also well stated it : —

> " Constant rotation of the unwearied wheel
>     That Nature rides upon maintains her health,
>     Her beauty, her fertility.   She dreads
>     An instant's pause, and lives but while she moves."

Long ago Plato said, " Everything mortal is preserved, not by its being in every respect the same
forever, but by the thing that is departing leaving

some new thing like itself," — and this is true, though every external form, everything possessed of the instinct of life, shrinks from this renewing power, distrusts the spirit, hardly believing that it can furnish a better habitation, fairer scenes, or more beautiful forms. To this persistent mutability and perpetual change we owe the idea of one spirit of humanity, one absolute order, one pervasive wisdom, one ruling mind. We see that no development is independent and alone; no condition has inherent force in itself; no being has essential permanence and life. All events are related and dependent; and all the doings of the race must be referred to a common unity, — one source of order and life, one inspiring spirit of humanity, one power accomplishing through infinite changes its vast designs.

To arrive at some final goal in truth and at complete happiness and well-being would bring to an end all development or progress, and so would be death. It is essential that an ideal goodness, beauty, truth, should still lure us on. Whatever form of these is attained will not completely satisfy, but as contrasted with that ideal will always appear to lack some perfection, and will at length be called evil, — and when it once comes into the consciousness as evil, its doom is sealed. To feel one's ignorance is the first step to knowledge; to feel one's imperfection is the beginning of a nobler life. So with social evils, or those institutions and general methods of life which are seen to work evil and not good to the organization that we call the commonwealth, — when once they are seen to be evils, there is no lasting peace until they are brought into harmony with the new and higher ideal. As that future is also the heir of the infinite, our present good may wear to it the form of evil.

The discoveries of our day in science and art are wonderful, but the ideas which underlie them are more wonderful still. Railway and telegraph are great as mechanical inventions, but greater in what they suggest and symbolize, — the intercommunication of national thought and life. How impossible for them to have existed in any known period of the past! What scope can there be for inventive genius under the protection of absolute power and the enslavement of man? What field for the free play of human faculties can exist among poor and ignorant masses, toiling for bare subsistence when they can be spared from the battle-field? What opportunity can be offered for combined action when there is no mutual confidence and trust? The external results and physical wonders of our era point to something higher than themselves, and are far more wonderful as indications than even as facts. They are a pledge of mental, moral, and spiritual conditions that must accompany the mechanical and external benefit.

In a recent book on " Power and Liberty," Tolstoï rightly calls history " a science of the movements of peoples and of humanity, not a description of episodes in the lives of a few men." In this light every human life is great, as sharing in the one life that manifests itself in every racial movement,—is infinitely little, when taken as a cause by itself, an independent factor or power. History is not the achievement of some few great men, but of all the men who make up at any one moment the living forces of human tendency. As a coral reef is the combined work of an infinity of living agents, so the social state at any point of time is the combination of all the forces embodied in the forms of living men and women; not one is so small as to be left out. When we have given up the study of the particular cause of this and that phenomenon in the vast world of phenomena which we call universal history, and seek simply for the manifested laws or methods of operation, we shall find that the social development is as truly a cosmos, a sphere of beautiful and harmonious order, as is this physical universe in which we struggle during our little day.

THE END.